# Advance Praise
## OTHER THAN THAT, I'M FINE

Judy Millar pokes fun at modern life, historical figures, marriage, aging, even death. Rib-tickling prose and poetry.

— Pat Smekal, poet and author of *Ripples, Small Corners,* and *Praise without Mortar*

*Other That That I'm Fine* is effortlessly and effervescently funny and Judy is Vancouver Island's answer to Erma Bombeck. Humour fans will love this new collection.

— Susan Juby, author of *A Meditation on Murder*

Through a delightfully skewed point of view, Judy breathes humour into a surprising variety of topics.

— Ian Cognitō, author of *Animusings*, editor of *Old Bones & Battered Book Ends* (Repartee Press)

# Other Than That, I'm Fine

## Essays on Life and Other Inconveniences

Judy Millar

This edition first published in 2024 by Brannen Publishing. Address inquiries to info@brannenpublishing.com.

Contact the author via her website: https://judymillar.ca.

978-0-9918177-0-2 (paperback)

978-0-9918177-2-6 (e-Book)

978-0-9918177-1-9 (hardcover)

Certain names and identifying details have been changed, whether or not so noted in the text.

Acknowledgement is made that some stories in this collection first appeared, some differently titled or in slightly different form, in print or online publications listed in the section titled Previous Publication Credits. In all cases, copyright remains with the author.

Cover & Author Photos: Barbara Anne Photography

https://barbaraanne.ca

Cover design by Bojan Reković @pixelstudio

Interior book design by Vellum

*For Corinne*
*and all who love to laugh*

# Contents

# HISTORICAL LIFE
## They Did Whaaat?

# MARRIED LIFE
## Dating, Mating & Relating

# END OF LIFE
## Aging, Death, That's All, Folks

# Introduction

Welcome!

Thank you for buying, borrowing, or even stealing this book to read. (Stealing is a crime, but in this case, who am I to judge?)

*Who, even, AM I?* Well, my name is Judy Millar (in case you missed it on the cover). I'm a longtime Canadian writer and sometimes comedic storyteller—as well as a one-time chicken plucker and professional puppeteer. No snickering. I doubt that you've been paid to put your arm up a sheep puppet's bum. It's honest work.

I'm southern Ontario born and bred, but I now call Vancouver Island home. I live with my husband (herein oft-maligned, but fondly forgiven) and two well-loved, disobedient dogs.

*Me?* I'd say I'm a klutzy 2 out of 10 mechanically and athletically, but an 8 out of 10 in hotness (#joke. Unless I'm wearing my Tommy Bahama red dress, then #nojoke.)

Mostly I'm just a senior woman living life, marvelling at its weirdness, and writing about it.

I hope you enjoy these essays, poems and true stories on the stuff of being alive. Some are new; others were penned as blog posts during the pandemic shutdown; a few have been scooped from my storytelling performances. (Check the "Video Performances" section of this book for online location information for my videos—and hyperlinks, if you're reading the eBook.)

I've loosely corralled this mashup of material into five sections:

HUMAN LIFE (Mine. And likely yours. We're all wonderfully weird, with our flaws and failings, quirks and idiosyncrasies, peeves and imperfections. *Hooray.* We're human!)

MODERN LIFE (Frappuccinos, Fitbits, phone-line limbo and other #%!# frustrations)

HISTORICAL LIFE (Featuring online dating profiles for famous historical figures and the "beefs" that wives of famous men may have had with their partners).

MARRIED LIFE (The mating, dating and relating game—including weird animal sexxx stuff!)

END OF LIFE (Aging and dying, including funny epitaphs of folks who got in the last word, and obituaries you can steal to leave 'em laughing).

***Dive right in, or cherry-pick your preferred section.*** Wherever you land, you'll be looking at life—mine, yours, everyone else's—through the lens of laughter, because we're all a bit of a mess. But, other than that, we're fine!

# LIFE

## Hooray! We're Human

# My Life as a "Live Wire"

I wasn't even surprised when my mother told me I was a breech birth. Right out of the gate, I was already a klutz.

I think I vaguely recall tumbling around *in utero*, trying to get the head part aimed down. My left knee had become hooked over my right elbow. Aiming my tush part out seemed like my only option. My em\*bare-ass\*ing entrance was only the first of many humiliations.

The world is not kind to us klutzes. Schoolyard team sports are a horror for us. *Dear God, please don't let me be picked last*, I'd pray with every new semester. I think I actually heard God chuckle. *AS IF.*

I eventually learned that the working world isn't any kinder to klutzes. To save for university, I found employment on an assembly line at a trailer factory. The camping craze was just catching on in the late-60s, and Rocket Trailers couldn't turn out their travel trailers fast enough. They certainly couldn't with me working on the assembly line.

I was assigned to work the electrical station. Given my own tool belt, wire strippers and screw drivers. That was the nature of the job: I had to strip the casing off of the wires, twist them together, attach a marrette, and screw the trailer's interior light fixtures into place. Naturally, the lust-addled guys on the line called us newbie-girls the "strippers" and "screwers." I was the worst stripper and screwer in the history of the trailer industry.

*Picture this*: Every few minutes, a big, burly guy would come and pull the trailer I was wiring ahead to the next station, a powered station. I would run alongside, begging to be let back in to finish screwing up—literally—my last light fixture or stove hood.

And those stove hoods were my nemesis. Asking an English major to wire your electrical appliance—that's like asking your ex if you can still be friends after your break-up. It's never going to work out.

But it taught me my first life lesson: *The black wire is always the hot wire.*

Unfortunately the red wire can sometimes be a secondary hot wire. In certain circumstances, even blue and yellow wires can be hot wires. Of course, I could never remember the "when" and "where" of it all.

Yes, I landed on my backside, and gained great respect for what 110 volts feels like when it travels through your body. A while later, I somehow managed to "ground myself" again.

That's when my foreman and I had a little talk. He was gentle. *Judy, we are not all equally suited to every job.*

With that, my life as a live wire came to an abrupt end. It's embarrassing to electrocute yourself once. I was terminated for winning the "daily double."

# Conveyor Belt Klutz

A klutz I may be, but I am no quitter. The factory floor was still the best place for a student with no appreciable skills to make some serious summer cash, so I made my way across town to J. M. Schneider meat processing plant. In their wisdom, they took me on in their poultry division.

I was thrilled. Plucking poultry sounded a lot safer than working with live wires. *The chicken was dead, so what could really happen?*

My new foreman said he'd start me on the sorting line. "You'll stand beside the conveyor belt and sort chicken pieces into groupings of three—a leg, a breast and a thigh—for our frozen dinner product," he explained.

That sounded easy enough. I could recognize a chicken leg, breast and thigh. *Count me in!*

But then he took me out onto the factory floor and set me up on the line. I saw that the chicken pieces were all being cooked in a giant cauldron-cooker, way up high. Suddenly an alarm sounded, and hundreds of chicken pieces spilled out of the cooker—*all jumbled together*—onto an inclined U-trough conveyor.

Then they thundered down toward us sorters! Our fingers flew as we sorted *leg, breast, thigh; leg, breast, thigh; leg, breast, thigh*, and watched our little groupings travel onward into the huge open mouth of a flash freezer.

One day I drew the position nearest to the flash freezer. My co-workers further up the line sweltered in the heat from the cooker, but I had to wear a ski jacket because the cold air flowing from the open door could actually freeze my upper arm.

Meanwhile, my right side was still hot from the heat and steam from the cooker. I took to leaving my ski jacket unzipped and tried to cool myself by flapping the jacket's right side. My new working rhythm was: *leg, breast, thigh; leg, breast, thigh;* ***flap, flap, flap***; *leg, breast thigh.*

Until . . . somehow, my "flapper" routine hooked my jacket's zipper tab into the conveyor belt's metallic mesh. *Suddenly I was being pulled along toward the flash freezer!*

My moves morphed into *leg, breast, thigh;* ***pull, yank, pull!*** But no matter how hard I pulled, I couldn't free that zipper tab.

I can still see myself, scrambling alongside that conveyor belt, tugging at the jacket's hem, screaming in panic. Soon, my co-workers were running alongside and screaming something too.

AT NO TIME did it occur to me to simply remove the jacket and let *it* proceed into the flash freezer. Because . . . we are not all equally suited to every job.

Turns out being flash-frozen hurts less than being electrocuted. But only because my foreman hit the panic button, stopped the line, and switched me from sorter to plucker.

# Breathe Like Brenda

U h-oh. I'm still awake. It's going to be one of those nights.

*No!* I'm not letting this happen. If I fall asleep *right now*, I can still get my seven hours. Okay, six and three-quarters hours. I think that's right. I was never good at math.

Not like Gloria Giesbrecht. I wonder what Gloria's doing now. Probably math equations for NASA. What have *I* done with *my* life?

***Stop it!*** *You were Employee of the Month.* Yes. In 2014. It's been a decade! *See, I CAN do math.* But what have I done *lately*?

I remembered to bring my own bag into the supermarket today. No more judgy looks from that cashier, what's-her-name. What *IS* her name? She's told me twice. I can almost picture it, there on her badge. Is this the start of Alzheimer's?

***Stop it!*** *You're overthinking it. Just BREATHE. Do the technique that yoga nut Brenda is always raving about—that alternate nostril breathing thing.*

Yes, just breathe like Brenda. How hard could it be? She said to inhale through your left nostril while closing your right, and then exhale through your right nostril, while closing your left.

*Hmm.* My left one's plugged. I'm not getting any air in. Brenda's nostrils must be bigger. Actually they are bigger. They're almost gross.

Also, she has that droopy eyelid. But she has great shoes. Brenda is the Imelda Marcos of shoes. I should've bought those red sandals I saw at Scooby Doo's Shoes. Brenda would've totally bought those. Great to distract from her nasty nostrils. *Ha!*

**Stop it!** That was mean. I should try her alternate nostril breathing technique again. Maybe reverse the order. Yes. Start with a right-nostril inhale. *There.*

Now exhale, left.

*Left is still plugged.*

Shelleen swears by her Neti pot to clear her nasal cavities. Should I get one of those?

No, didn't the FDA say improper use of Neti pots can lead to infections, including the deadly Naegleria fowleri?

Why can I remember "Naegleria fowleri," when I can't even recall that cashier's name!

**Stop it!** *Her name will come to you. But you know you'd never figure out how to use a Neti pot. You'd have brain-eating amoeba in no time.*

I might already have brain-amoeba already since I keep forgetting names.

What if I stick to *right* nostril breathing, and just exhale through my mouth?

Yes. That works better for me.

But now my right foot is tingling. Why is my foot asleep, when the rest of me is still awake!

Why am I the only one who can't sleep . . .

***Stop it!*** *There are lots of insomniacs. They manage. Didn't George Clooney say he struggles with insomnia?* I wouldn't mind being awake if George was awake beside me.

I guess Amal would mind, though. I wonder how their marriage is holding up since the twins. He's not likely to step out on her—she's quite striking.

Although, I heard she had a nose job. Maybe *I* should have rhinoplasty? Then I'd be able to alternate-nostril breathe like Brenda, and I'd never need a Neti pot . . .

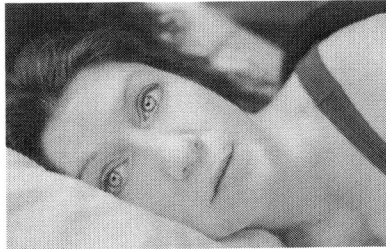

# My Eye Guy is On To Me

I am not a cheater. Not exactly. As a student, I earned every one of my dismal Math marks. I pay every penny of my taxes. I am wholly monogamous (or mostly, if you can allow for a few George Clooney fantasies). And yet . . . I cheat on eye tests.

Why? Because I can. Or rather, I could.

It used to be easy. As easy as DEFPOTEC. That was the line for 20/20 vision on the eye chart my optometrist used for years. I'd memorized those letters back in school, camped out in the nurse's office. I could still spit them out like Kalashnikov bullets, although I shrewdly offered them up in a halting, Oscar-worthy performance: Uhh **D**, **E**, *is that an* **F**?—yes **F**, um-**P**?

DEFPOTEC, and his upper line buddy FELOPZD, worked for me for years.

But those years flew by. Eventually, some pesky issues cropped up that got me referred to a full-fledged ophthalmologist. My new eye guy's office had sleek, Scandinavian furniture and abstract paintings on the walls. *Or did they only LOOK abstract due to my failing eyesight?* I felt a tingle of perspiration bloom on my brow.

The receptionist ushered me into an exam room and got me settled. I scanned the walls. *No eye chart?* Turns out my new guy had splurged on more than Scandinavian furniture.

He'd purchased a digital eye chart projector that rotated a bewildering array of eye chart choices and projected lines of their letters onto the blank wall. My old friends DEFPOTEC and his sidekick FELOPZD were nowhere to be seen. Now, the only thing I saw clearly was a pair of progressive lenses in my immediate future.

Then "new guy" sprang another surprise on me. "I think it's time you took the Humphrey test," he said.

The *Humphrey* test? I gave him my best Bogart imitation: *"Here's looking at you, kid!"*

Eye Guy frowned. "It's not a movie trivia test. It's a visual field test."

A visual field test? *Hmm.* I might be able to find some Humphrey-beating tricks on the internet.

"Uhh. Can I cram for it and take it next week?"

My old guy would have laughed at that. New guy just rolled his eyes. *You'd think an ophthalmologist would know better.*

*"Won't rolling wreck your retinas?"*

He ignored that, and sent me down the hall to a little room with a huge machine operated by an equally no-nonsense technician. She placed a pirate patch over my left eye and positioned my chin on a chin rest.

"Now keep your open eye fixed on the light in the centre of this screen," she said, placing a clicker in my hand. "Click this whenever you see a blinking light anywhere."

*Whaaaat??* Blinking lights will be coming at me? Decades of my life immediately vanish. My old Pac-Man[1] panic kicks in.

Once again I am a bright yellow circle who's chomping on dots as I play the Pac-Man game in a noisy arcade. Which might be fun, except that those little enemy ghosts—Inky, Blinky, Pinky, and Clyde—are coming at me! TO KILL ME. Aaaghh. There's Pinky now, upper quadrant! *Click.* Now Inky —lower right! *Click, click.* OMG. Was that Clyde?? *Click. Click! CLICK!*

I'm sweating now, and my ears are buzzing with that Pac-man *Waka Waka* sound I hate. *AAGGGH!*

"Calm down!" says the startled technician. "You're getting trigger-happy. Just fix your eye on that little light in the centre; stop looking all around the screen."

"I don't want to die . . . I mean, I don't want to miss any," I say, a pulse pounding in my ears.

"You're cheating," she says firmly. "This machine can tell."

She goes on to explain how this machine has been intricately calibrated to monitor gaze and detect straying eyeballs. It's very complex, but one thing is clear. I'm busted. Clyde is closing in. He has me in his crosshairs! I'm a goner!!

GAME OVER

# Lawdy, Lawdy: What a Body!

**W**e women are forever grumbling about our bodies. *My face is too long. My boobs are too small. My butt is too big. Yada. Yada.*

And yet . . . I recently read Bill Bryson's fascinating book, *The Body: A Guide for Occupants,* and realized our bodies are freaking amazing.

Bryson covers pretty much all our parts in a book that's like the Owner's Manual God forgot to include. *Did you know:*

## Your brain has shrunk

Don't take this personally. It's not the sort of sudden shrinkage Seinfeld's George Costanza suffered after a dip in the pool. Still, Bryson says your brain would have been 150 cubic centimetres larger if you'd been born 10,000 years ago.

Either—like an iPhone 12 Mini—you're packing more performance into your smaller package, or else you're just getting dimmer. You decide.

# Your lungs are l o o o n g

Smoothed out, Bryson estimates they would cover a tennis court. And the airways within them would stretch nearly from coast to coast.

Presumably your lungs wouldn't work as well when stretched from Bakersfield to Boston, so don't attempt to confirm this statistic on your own.

# Your saliva is copious

You'll secrete over 31,000 quarts of the stuff over the course of your life—enough to fill two hundred bathtubs. And get this: it contains opiorphin, a natural painkiller that's six times more potent than morphine.

Sadly, you produce so little of it that spit-harvesting in hopes of becoming the next drug kingpin would be a bad career move.

# Your hair is "hair today, gone tomorrow"

You'll grow some 25 feet of hair in your lifetime, but you lose between 50 and 100 hairs a day. Bryson says about sixty percent of males are "substantially bald" by the age of 50.

Happily, there is a cure. But you've got to really want it. Castration is not for everyone.

# You eat and excrete tons

Over your lifetime, you'll eat some 60 tons of food—and turn it into seven tons of poop. Then there's the accompanying flatulence. One poor dude in France came to an explosive end when doctors attempted to cauterize his rectal polyp.

You are unlikely to suffer a similar fate thanks to improved laparoscopic techniques. Still, I wouldn't swing by Taco Bell en route to your colonoscopy.

## Your end is not "The End"

"A corpse is very much alive. It's just not *your* life any longer."

— Bill Bryson

Your bacteria quickly combine with others that flock in to create new gases and compounds. If that sounds like less fun than you're having in the form you currently occupy, get busy and enjoy your body while you can!

Bryson also digs into what happens when we do just that— exploring the physiology behind fun stuff like kissing.

Got the sniffles? No worries. Kissing is the *least* effective way to spread cold germs, he says. You and your main squeeze may swap a billion bacteria while canoodling, but as soon as the party's over, he says the host microorganisms of both of you start "sweeping-out" the bad guys.

If we've only got one life to live inside these awesome bodies, I say: *Pucker up, and live it up!*

# Hey, Chuck Gobnik!

As if the nightly news isn't enough to get on my nerves, now it's the news**casters** who are driving me nuts. Yes, I'm peevish about pronunciation. Is there not a "talking head" on TV who can correctly pronounce the N-word?

Not *THAT* N-word. Nobody should be saying that. I mean the OTHER N-word. I've been trying to tell my local guy: **It's not nuc-U-lar, dammit!**

*Check the spelling, Chuck.* Is there a *U* after the *C* in **nuclear**? There is not. That's why nuclear is pronounced with an *E: NEW-cl**ee**-er.* Don't they teach catastrophically-critical words in broadcasting school anymore, Chuck ? Oh, you were away that day.

Well, listen up. "Nuc**u**lar" relates to a "nucule," or nut. *No wonder it drives me nuts.* "Nucl**e**ar" pertains to the nucleus of a cell. It's atomic, not botanic, Chuck! So lose that *U* before I go all nuclear on *U!*

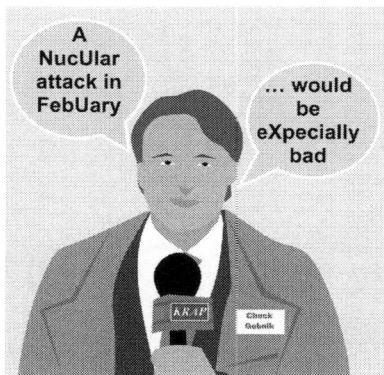

## Feb U ary: Where'd you chuck the "R," Chuck?

Now, about February. You can't just go ditching consonants on a whim, buddy. You'll pull down the ire of the gods. Specifically the Roman god Feb-RU-us, who got his name from Feb-RU-a, the Roman festival of purification.

Yes, I am a Pronunciation Purist, Chuck. In fact, I am a proud member of the PPL, the *Pronunciation Purification League*. We are legion—think Roman legion, Chuck. You will *RU* the day you messed with the PPL, so add in that *R* in February. And BTW . . .

## The polar region is not called the Artic

There are two Cs in Ar**c**tic, Chuck—possibly because it's very *c-c*old up there—so quit dropping #1! You say it feels weird on your tongue to say that first C? Yes, it's tricky to press the back of your tongue against the back of your soft palate, but that's why you're a professional, Chuck. You get paid to do the tongue tricks!

*What's that?* Did you just say, "It's expecially hard to say Arctic when your mouth is dry"?

## There's no "X" in "especially," Chuck!

And, no, I will NOT get you an eXpresso for your dry mouth. There's no X in "espresso" OR in "especially," man. *Why do you always stick in an X?*

You say it's because you can't forget your Ex? Surely you're not still hung up on Hilda? She put you through hell, man! You say you still love her? What do you mean, you're going to "axe" her out again? There's no X in "ask," Chuck!

Also, that's a VERY BAD idea. You've got to lose these Xs, man. Lose every one of them.

*"Including Hilda?"*

"EXpecially, Hilda!"

*"I thought you said — "*

"That was a JOKE, Chuck. *A JOKE.*"

# To the Cliché Cops in My Writing Group

*ear Snooty Simon, Condescending Carol and Annoying Everyone Else:*
**D**I won't beat around the bush. I have an axe to grind and I'm ready to blow a gasket. I'm mad as a hornet and I'm not going to take it anymore.

You're all over my clichés like white on rice, saying I should avoid them like the plague. Well, it may come as a bolt out of the blue, but you are throwing out the baby with the bathwater.

I think a canned cliché can be as good as new when a picture's worth a thousand words. For example, addressing "the elephant in the room" could slyly imply Carol's packed on a few pounds. No offence, Carol.

I do agree we shouldn't go overboard with clichés. When you kiss the cat, you catch its fleas and those could breed like rabbits, to mix a metaphor.

Speaking of breeding, is *that* the reason you've been plumping up, Carol? Another bun in the oven? Oops-a-daisy. My bad for spilling the beans! Mum's the word from here on out.

And Simon: I reject your premise that clichés are the lazy sloths of literature. Although I acknowledge that your very original line about the sky being as blue as Lysol in the bowl has stuck like TP in the bowl of my brain, impossible to flush away.

I would, however, argue that originality is overrated. It may even be undetected plagiarism, as noted by writer Herbert Paul in 1896—which is THREE FULL YEARS before the invention of Lysol, I'm just saying. Clearly there is nothing new under the sun.

You all claim you're sick to death of my clichés, but what doesn't kill you makes you stronger (just ask Kelly Clarkson!). My bite-sized bits of eternal wisdom may be just what the doctor ordered.

All that glitters is not gold, but clichés are definitely diamonds, polished over centuries. And they're a girl's best friend when her Muse has gone missing.

I can take criticism as well as the next guy (certainly better than Carol, who's still snivelling because I spilled her little secret—for crying out loud, Carol!). Still, I'm at my wits' end with you kvetching cliché cops.

The correct cliché can make chicken soup out of chicken poop, as some of you might see if you sprinkled a few into your sub-par poems.

Let me just lay it on the line here: I challenge any one of you to come up with a phrase half as enduring as the clichés you keep criticizing.

Will people still be calling the sky "Lysol blue" in 2052, Simon!? Well, until then, I refuse to kill my darlings, *DAHLINGS*.

# An Ode to Parentheticals

I think in parentheses. The bracket, dash and comma keys on my keyboard are concussed from so many hits to their little heads. Unfortunately, one of my editors can't stand parentheses. I couldn't resist getting my Ogden Nash on, and writing this wee poem for Susan:

> I hate to be heretical
> But I LIKE parentheticals
> I dig that they're symmetrical
> And find them quite aesthetical
>
> This may sound theoretical
> But here's a hypothetical:
> Is Susan's peeve p'raps medical?
> A syndrome that's genetical

*That renders her frenetical*
*At sightings parenthetical*
*'Til she becomes a spectacle*
*That's driven apoplectical?*

*We must be sympathetical*
*If her condition's medical*
*That's why I'm empathetical*
*In this wee verse poetical.*

# Here's Looking at You, Whoever You Are

Some people claim they never forget a face. I rarely remember one until I've encountered it repeatedly. Ideally in the same location or context. (If I once met you on the ski hill, please never remove your helmet.)

As a teenager, I began to notice that my girlfriends could identify every teen idol in the magazine. Meanwhile The Beatles, with their identical mop-tops, were a mishmash for me (although I swore I adored Paul, because who didn't?).

Years later, I was pretty sure I was falling in love with a guy I'd met at the roller rink. Did it matter that whenever a week passed before I saw him again, his facial features had evaporated from my mind?

*He has a beard*, I'd think. *He's tall. Lanky.*

My mind pulled up a stock photo of Abraham Lincoln. From then on, in my mind, I was dating Honest Abe. Honest Abe on roller-skates.

Eventually "Abe" morphed into a man I could picture and I married him. But my "condition" hasn't improved over the years.

It's led to many-an-awkward moment after speaking events. More and more people seem to know me. They approach afterward, eager to chat. They act as if we go way back. For all I know, we do.

"I'm Hannah," that face might say, looking at me oddly. "You know, we talked last week about our hernias." I slap my forehead then, hoping to imply I've only blanked on her name, not our whole herniated history.

I'd almost convinced myself this was normal. Then I spotted an article in the *Washington Post Magazine*: "My Life with Face Blindness."

Its author, Sadie Dingfelder, stated she was startled to learn that "face blindness" is a legitimate neurological condition. She underwent testing which confirmed her brain won't let her easily recognize people. She suffers from prosopagnosia, or face blindness. One in every 50 people share this disorder. I had a lightbulb moment: OMG. I am a prosopagnosiac.

I like my new label, even if I can't pronounce it. I can finally stop beating myself up over the fuzzy faces on my mental screen.

An artist friend scoffs at my self-diagnosis. "Nonsense," she says. "Just try dividing a face into quadrants and map out its features.

"As in, *Linda's lip slopes southwest?*" I joke.

She rolls her eyes. "Okay. Maybe just memorize ONE unique feature."

I've begun experimenting with that at social gatherings. But how do you carry on a conversation while trying to memorize a peculiarity? "That's so nose—I mean nice," I might say to Frank with the flaring nostrils.

Already he's morphed into Jimmy Durante in my mind. (My brain tends to cheat by assigning celebrity lookalikes.) Next time, I'll probably call him Jim.

I can only hope I never witness an armed robbery and have to identify the criminal. I marvel at people who can confidently describe a culprit to a police sketch artist: *No, his eyes were closer together and he had a weaker chin*, they might say.

Unless my perpetrator is Jay Leno, whose colossal jaw I still recognize from years of watching *The Tonight Show*, I'll be no help.

Another celebrity who apparently shares my condition is Brad Pitt. And Brad has actually said he'd like to meet me. Well, sort of. He recently discussed his prosopagnosia on CNN, and said, "I wanna meet another [person with it]."

*Here I am, Brad! Over here!*

Brad complains his face-blindness makes people think he's aloof and self-absorbed, when he actually isn't. The disorder makes him dislike going out in public—a real handicap for a celebrity. "You meet so many damned people," he groused in *Esquire*. "And then you meet 'em again!"

I totally get it. And it's kind of cool that we have this condition in common. Although he's a multi-millionaire. He's even got a villa in Majorca. I'd rather we had that in common.

Just imagine. He'd have his villa. I'd have mine. There we'd be, passing each other on the street every day—forever strangers, exchanging puzzled, prosopagnosic glances, then walking on by.

But we'd be *in Majorca*. How cool is that!

# MODERN LIFE

## Your Call Is Important to Us

# Fitbitten: Who, Me?

I'm not what you'd call competitive. Not exactly.

Okay. There've been moments. In my past. Like when I bent Hilda Kehler's halo because she got to be Mary in the Christmas pageant instead of me. I'm not proud of messing with the Virgin Mary. But I was young. Plus I was a donkey, so what can you expect?

I've matured with age. Now I try to be less of an ass. Mostly I succeed. But last Christmas I got a Fitbit.

My daughter-in-law had been raving about tracking her physical activity on what looked to me like a plastic toy watch. She said it gave her a wrist-tingle when she hit her goal of 10,000 steps a day. Fireworks exploded on its screen. She had me at wrist-tingle.

I needed a watch that watched *me*. One that applauded me for plodding through my day. One that celebrated my successes.

Santa delivered.

Ten thousand steps a day turned out to be a challenge for a sedentary writer, but I pushed through until I felt my first wrist-prickle. Fireworks detonated across my Fitbit's screen. Imaginary crowds in the stands roared their approval. I was hooked.

From then on, I wore my Fitbit everywhere. I even wore it to a formal dance (it clashed with my glitzy gown, but I wanted every rumba to register).

I loved flaunting my Fitbit in front of my friends. "I need to check my numbers," I'd say casually. They'd roll their eyes. I didn't care. My step-count was climbing. I soon got a notification from Fitbit:

> Congratulations! With 70 lifetime miles, you've earned your 'March of the Penguins' Badge.

OMG. I'd marched as far as emperor penguins march to get to their breeding grounds!

I couldn't resist gloating. I texted my daughter-in-law:

> What should I do now? Breed a new baby brother for your hubby? Ha ha.

She gave me an LOL, and one-upped me:

> Your Penguin badge is peanuts.

Turned out she'd just earned her Giraffe badge. She'd walked the 500-mile distance of the Serengeti. Giraffes trump Penguins. This penguin was pissed.

I had to up my count—and quick—if I was ever to outdo that smug giraffe.

My baser nature kicked in.

Somewhere in my distant past, a donkey brayed, then whispered in my ear: *What if you exaggerate your wrist movements while typing?*

Soon, every time I hit the spacebar, my wrist lurched sideways, then snapped back down. Done just right, it netted me some extra steps. Yes!

When I came down with a cold, a braying in my brain said: *Why not fasten your Fitbit to your shih tzu's collar?* My dog-walker never even noticed. When the dog later took to his mat, I hooked the Fitbit onto my metronome. *Tick-tock—take a walk.*

My step count was climbing—*hee haw!*—but so was my guilt. Legit workouts were called for. When fitness classes didn't get me to my goal, I added country line dancing and racked up some serious steps doing redneck aerobics to the beat of Billy Ray Cyrus.

It worked. Fitbit told me I'd earned my "London Underground Badge." I'd walked the length of the world's first underground railway! Fitbit applauded:

> This really lays the tracks for big triumphs in the future.

I made tracks to tell the giraffe. She smiled and said she was no longer strolling the Serengeti. While I'd been stuck in the London Underground, she'd perambulated all of "Italy"! Plus, she'd earned her "Cowboy Boot Badge" for 50,000 steps taken on one all-day hike.

No fair! I'd been hoofing it with the King of Country Music, and I only got my lousy "Urban Boot Badge." My Achy Breaky Heart broke. There was no catching her.

"Let's end this silly competition," she suggested.

"You're right," I said. "We're being juvenile."

We hugged on it. I patted her back warmly. Only a jackass would have checked her wrist to see if those pats registered.

# Half-baked Barista

*You want a*
half-caf, no whip
Frap
in a Venti cup?

Apple Crisp
Oatmilk?
Sure 'nuff
Comin' right up.

Cappuccino
Frappuccino
Al Pacino ...
*Bro, we got it!*

*Your order was a . . .*
*well, it kinda*
*slipped my mind.*
*I just forgot it*

*Was it a*
Very Berry, full-caf
4-pump, sugar-free
Skinny?

*Or else a*
Double Splenda, Sun-dried
Clover-caf
from Papua New Guinea?

*Was it a*
6 pump, Italian-iced
Shakerato
— skip the stir?

*I'm kinda blitzed*
*from last night, man.*
*My brain's*
*a blur*

*You say a*
half-caf, no whip
Frap — Apple Oat?
*We sell that ...*

*Now, I think you said*
*your name was Bob ...*
*Buddy,*
*how d'ya spell that?*

# Naughty Lattes

## Limericks, Starbucks style

### Siren Call
*A Starbucks barista named Byron*
*Mesmerized by the coffee cup's Siren*
*Daydreamed he got laid*
*By the twin-tailed mermaid.*
*Instead he got canned. Now they're hirin'.*

### Hit Me Again, Dino
*A Starbucks barista named Dino*
*Was known for his mean Frappuccino*
*His customers tasted*
*And promptly got wasted*
*'Cause Dino liked adding some vino.*

### Gotcha, Matcha

*A Starbucks barista trainee*
*Was making a Matcha Green Tea*
*She poured in the water*
*Which should have been hotter*
*Her customer got it for free.*

### Boo Hoo, Buster

*A Starbucks barista named Buster*
*Was known for his Cocoa Frap Cluster*
*His inamorato*
*Loved Cloud Macchiato*
*So Buster could never pass muster.*

### Oh Boy, Roy

*A Starbucks barista named Roy*
*Was asked for a latte with soy*
*His customer swallowed*
*Cacophony followed*
*'Cause Roy substituted bok choy.*

### Pay up, Patrons

*A Starbucks barista named Pink*
*Gave limericks free with each drink.*
*The owner said, "See here!*
*There's nothing for free here!*
*Each rhyme's worth a dime, don't cha think?"*

# Your Call Is (he, he) Important to Us

Y our call is important to them? *Riiight.*

Thank you for your patience your call is important to us.

Drawn while on phone to insurance company for 42 mins

*Your call is important to us. Please stay on the line until your call is no longer important to you.*

— Andrew Fraser on X (used by permission)

*What number do I press to speak to an actual human,* you wonder, as you pound the zero button, to no avail. The days when an actual switchboard operator welcomed you warmly and promptly put you through are long gone.

I had fun picturing today's Interactive Voice Response system as an old-timey switchboard operator in this satirical performance piece.

Full script below.

*Under the right circumstances, all women can be dangerous. But there is only one woman who can drive you to the brink of madness in a matter of minutes—and you have met her. She sounds so sweet ... so sunny ... so upbeat ... as she whispers in your ear:*

AUTOMATED VOICE:
Thank you for your call. For service in English, Press 1. Pour le service en français, faîtes le deux.

**I'm the Automated Lady
And I'm here to drive you crazy.
Help me redirect your call;
Let me drive you up the wall.**

If you know your account number, please enter it now.
If you don't know your account number, press #POUND, and prepare to enter Purgatory. (*pause*) We are experiencing higher than usual call volume in Purgatory. Some souls have been lost in this limbo since the Clinton administration.

"There's nothing wrong with you that reincarnation won't cure" seems equally harsh. (But clever.)

> *There's nothing wrong with you that reincarnation won't cure.*
>
> — Jack E. Leonard

At best, I might be able to get my "Groucho" on, and sneer, "I've had a perfectly wonderful evening. I'm afraid this wasn't it."

> *I've had a perfectly wonderful evening. I'm afraid this wasn't it.*
>
> — Groucho Marx

Feel free to borrow any of those witty barbs to stand up for yourself. Unfortunately, in the heat of the moment, I can never remember any clever comebacks. It's taken me 70 years to learn that, for me, the best reaction to receiving an unexpected verbal "slap," is to state the simple truth:

"Ouch. That hurt."

It's surprising how often a perpetrator will be stung and shamed into back-pedalling—"I *didn't mean that like it sounded*"—if I can land these three simple words *immediately*.

"Ouch. That hurt" can even sometimes open up a respectful conversation that helps resolve a deeper issue ("Sorry. All I meant was . . . "). Even if it doesn't, I feel better for having made a quick, candid comeback. At least I won't have to stew about my speechlessness at 2 a.m.

**I'm the Automated Lady
And I'm here to drive you crazy.**

If you're calling for store hours and locations, press 1.
If you're calling for your account balance, press 2.
If you're calling to try to . . . fix that screw-up on your account,
*he he*. . . please enter the Secret PIN number we sent you last
January.
If you've forgotten your secret PIN number (*eye roll*), shame on
you, and please press *STAR. Pressing *STAR will redirect you
to the Twilight Zone. We are experiencing extremely high call
volume in the Twilight Zone.
To thank you for your patience, we will now drop you into an
endless loop of John Denver singing "Rocky Mountain High."
If you would prefer to listen to Gordon Lightfoot singing
"Sundown," press #POUND to return to Purgatory.

**I'm the Automated Lady
And I'm here to drive you crazy.**

Thank you for your patience. Your call is important to us. All
our calls are answered in sequence. Please stay on the line to
hold your place in the queue. We are now serving customers
who called in the aftermath of 9–11. If you would like to be
transferred to a real live Customer Service Representative
(*hehe*) . . . that is, if you would like to be transferred to a
Customer Service Representative who actually gives a crap,
you could try pressing zero. *It won't work, but you could try.*

I wouldn't advise pressing zero though. It pisses me off when
people press zero . It's like they don't appreciate the efforts I go
to, to keep my voice syrupy-sweet ... and to enunciate the

choices clearly ... and to learn all these different languages, so I can say ...
... Pour le service en français
and
... Para español, oprima el numero tres ...

Do you think it's easy learning all this shit? Well, do you?
How about you try it, while you're juggling Gordon Lightfoot and John Denver tapes!
And do you think it's easy trying to keep my cool when some hothead like you is listening to me recite my choices, and telling me to eff-off?! You think I don't hear that? *I'm recording that!* You think that doesn't hurt my feelings? I have feelings! And I know how to get even.

**I'm the Automated Lady**
**And I LIVE to drive you crazy.**
**Go ahead! Try pressing 3**
**You sorry S-O-B.**
**I'll just dump you off this line!** (click) . .

**There! That's better. I feel fine**
**Now I got that off my chest;**
**Time to go deal with the rest . . .**
**There are hundreds more like you**
**Trying to move up in the queue.**
**We appreciate your call.**
**Thank you, one and all!**

# On Searching for Your Mobile Phone

*You check on the counter*
*and look in your purse*
*You feel down the sofa*
*and take time to curse*
*You clear off the desktop*
*and look in the drawer*
*You pull back the bedspread*
*and study the floor*
*You're starting to freak out —*
*it couldn't be far!*
*If it's not in the house*
*it must be in the car*
*You check down the car seat*
*still can't find a thing*
*You call from a landline*
*and feel your butt ring.[1]*

# What I Should Have Said Was . . .

Will Smith's slap of Chris Rock at the Oscars was heard around the world. But sometimes people slap us across the face with their rude words or snide comments (e.g., "You look good for a woman your age"), and we're rendered speechless.

I was never good at snappy comebacks. But oh, at 2:00 a.m. ...

## What I should have said was . . .

Some of the world's quickest wits were faster than Federer at lobbing a verbal burn. I've considered modifying a few of their snarkiest insults to use as snappy comebacks. Could I ever bring myself to respond, "Oh yeah? Well, your mother should have thrown you away and kept the stork!" ? Probably not.

*His mother should have thrown him away and kept the stork.*

— Mae West

That's when I'll be able to snicker to myself:

*There's nothing wrong with her that reincarnation won't cure.*

— Me

# Eve's Feminist Manifesto

*"Adam," said Eve, "it's not fair;*
*You must turn a new leaf, or beware.*
*I don't give a fig*
*For your thing-a-ma-jig*
*I want salary and perks that compare."*

# Tatyana Wants to Talk

Tatyana wants to talk. So does Anastasiya. And Yuliya. Lately I'm a chick magnet for hot babes from Russia.

Earnest invites to chat have been popping up on my MacBook's screen. Siberian bosoms have been bursting onto terrain I reserve for cat videos and Anderson Cooper's *coronavirus town hall*. And each pouty Muscovite mouth says it only wants to talk.

"You've been ad-jacked," says my friend Carol. "They think you're a horny western male. Whatever you do, don't click! And get yourself better Antivirus software."

I intend to. And yet, I've kind of taken to Tatyana. She's not as tough-looking as Yuliya.

*Did that eyebrow piercing hurt, honey? I'd soak that sucker in saline.*

Tatyana just looks sweet. And sort of lonely. Like someone who might really *want* to talk. I'll bet she's on lockdown in Moscow, going just as Covid-crazy as I am.

I'm tempted to click and kick off a conversation.

"Where'd you get that great studded bikini?" I'll ask for starters. "Can you actually swim in that? Wouldn't you sink?"

But then she might ask what *I'm* wearing. It would come out that she's a hot young chick and I'm a tracksuit-clad female on the wrong side of 70. She's a devushka. I'm a babushka.

Better to stick to stuff we might have in common. *The internet!* We both hang out on the internet.

"Are you goofing off too?" I'll ask. "When I should be writing, I'm always clicking around looking for cool stuff to buy. Yesterday I found a tin labelled 'Canned Unicorn Meat' on Ebay. What a great gag gift for my vegan friends!"

But that might get lost in translation.

"Do you know the term 'vegan,' Tatyana? *Vegitarianskiy?* It means people who don't eat meat — especially not unicorns! *Ha ha.*

She probably won't get it. International communication is a challenge. And if she struggles with English, my Russian won't be any help.

I studied it briefly. That Cyrillic script is a tricky bastard. The "B" sounds like "Vuh," the H" sounds like "Nuh," and the "P" sounds like "R-r-ruh." To which I finally said: WTF. And flunked out.

We'll have to use Google Translate and hope for the best.

"About Covid," I'll say. "Are things as bad as over there as they are here?"

"Da," she'll say. (Or "Nyet," if Putin's making them put out a positive spin.)

I'll press her for the real scoop. "I heard your Olympic ice dancing champion's come down with coronavirus. What's her name? Tatyana Something . . .wait ... Tatyana Navka, right?"

"Da," she'll say. "DA!"

"*Another* Tatyana," I'll say. "Seems like you're all named Tatyana!"

We'll share a girl-friendy chuckle then. Hitting it off like bosom buddies! (Although our bosoms are not remotely similar.)

But just as I'm about to click to cement our friendship, there's a *ding*. Another pop-up. And another. *And another.*

It's Alina. And Kristina. And Dominika. (So they're NOT all named Tatyana.)

And you would NOT BELIEVE the get-up on Dominika. That's just not right. Not on the same screen Anderson Cooper has to inhabit in half an hour. (He would be totally traumatized. And him just a new dad.)

Nope. I'm breaking it off. It's over between me and Tatyana.

I'm off to buy Antivirus.

# Hey, Morgan Freeman

My husband is not one to come home from Costco empty-handed, but this time he's outdone himself. He brought home a new girlfriend and installed her in our kitchen!

As women go, she's not taking up a lot of space. She's claimed a small corner of the countertop, setting up shop inside his newly purchased *Google Nest* home automation system.

Like the perfect 1950s housewife, this gal knows her place. Tucked away within the Nest's digital display screen, she speaks only when spoken to, yet stands ready to respond to her master's every whim.

"Hey Google, give me directions to Costco," he says to test her.

I wish she'd give him some lip: *Surely your vehicle knows the way by heart?*

But no.

She complies so sweetly it's like she's hoping he'll take her along back to her old stomping grounds so she can kibitz with the other *Google Nests* on her Costco shelf.

I want to try bossing someone around too, but I don't like the idea of barking orders at a female assistant. I open the Google Home app and switch over to a male voice. I'd heard there were celebrity voice options but these male voice choices all sound like robots.

*Darn.* I wanted to boss around a male celebrity. Someone with a deep commanding voice to respond to my wishes with the right amount of gravitas. Someone like Morgan Freeman!

Who better than God to respond to my every whim!? Well, *actual* God would be better, but Morgan's played God so many times he must have picked up some omniscience along the way.

I load a Freeman photo onto the Nest screen and put my new Google Assistant through his paces.

*Hey Morgan, what's today's weather forecast?*

God's voice still sounds robotic— it's definitely not velvety — but Morgan's comforting face on the screen reassures me he has no plan to rain down a plague of locusts. No pests or pestilence lined up till at least the weekend.

I decide to make him up his game.

*Hey Morgan, turn up the heat and dim the dining room lights.*

My wish is his command. He even offers to turn the dining room light green!

*Not now, Morgan, but that'll be a fun party trick to try out on dinner guests. Tonight we're serving Duck à l'Orange **à la Green**!*

Ever the polite Canadian, I thank him for his flashy miracles with the house lights.

*I'm here to help. It's one of my favourite things to do.*

WHOA. Millionaire Morgan Freeman apparently LOVES serving a nobody like me. Well, game on!

*Hey Morgan Freeman, can you bark like a dog?*

"This is what a dog sounds like," he replies, and emits a convincing series of shrill barks. Startled, my shih tzu responds with indignant territorial barking.

Unperturbed by the racket, Morgan surprises me with a proposal.

*Would you like to hear the Animal of the Day?*

Er . . . Yes . . .

*Today's animal is the wombat. A group of wombats is known as a wisdom. Due to their long digestive process, which can take up to 18 days, and the lack of muscle contraction in their rectum, wombats leave cube-shaped scat.*

Shiiit. Did I really need to know all that? I guess omniscient assistants can't resist oversharing.

I try to catch him up on a trick question:

"Hey Morgan, who put the Bomp in the Bomp-bah Bomp-bah Bomp?"

*Now playing 'Who Put The Bomp' by Barry Mann on YouTube Music.* The music rolls.

I've had enough of this.

"Hey Morgan, take the night off!"

*Playing "Take the Night Off" by Laura Marling on YouTube Music.*

AAGGH. I should have known.

God never sleeps.

# Bidet, Mate!

When the Covid-19 crisis hit, panicked shoppers sought safety behind the flimsiest of fortifications: toilet paper. Never one to follow the hoarding herd, my guy rushed out to buy . . . a bidet.

"Toilet paper is passé," he announced as he unpacked the portable manual unit. "Why wipe, when a quick whoosh of water can bathe our back-ends?"

An hour later our run-of-the-mill bathroom throne was pimped out with a side-mounted seat attachment. A sort of stick shift for our ceramic Roadster.

*Take a seat*, it beckoned. *Enjoy a car wash for your booty.*

I've driven through a few car washes in my day so I was in no hurry to experience a deluge "Down Under." Still, that Aussie thought had me calling out a cheery "Bidet, Mate!" every time I was in the Roadster's vicinity.

*Bidet, yourself!* it seemed to reply. *C'mon, sissy. Take me for a spin.*

Eventually curiosity got the best of me. Time for a test drive.

I positioned my posterior on the seat and studied the gearshift lever warily. I hadn't driven a four-on-the-floor since I learned to drive in my dad's old Maverick. Presumably the unlabelled dots on this gizmo ranged from low to high, or maybe from "Tickle" to "Turbo."

Cautiously I shifted into first. A jolt of icy water nailed my right cheek. *"It's COLD,"* I yelled, jumping clear.

"The warm-water model cost more," my guy hollered from the hallway. "I got us the redneck version."

I glowered at him through the closed door, then glanced back at the offender.

*You fall off a horse, you get back on,* it sneered. *Don't be a wimp.*

Wimp or not, I wasn't about to turn the other cheek. Instead I decided to search the Roadster's reviews on Amazon. Surely I wasn't the only dissatisfied driver.

To my surprise, there were some glowing testimonials. *Sprays right on target!* enthused a reviewer who's clearly a better operator than yours truly. *Didn't splash my dangly bits,* he added, clearly relieved.

Most complaints came from homes with high water pressure. *Feels like a firehose on your fanny,* grumbled one drenched customer. *Don't dial up too fast or you'll power-wash your privates,* warned a survivor who claimed to be suffering from PTSD.

*More like PTTD—post-traumatic TUSH disorder—*I thought. I was glad I hadn't geared up to Turbo.

While I continued to give the bidet a wide berth, my guy could barely contain his enthusiasm. "I feel Springtime-Fresh!" he'd tell me every time he took the Roadster out for a spin.

"I don't care if daffodils are growing out of your derrière!" I shot back. "I'm sick of that thing smirking at me every time I tinkle. Park your jalopy elsewhere."

Happy wife, happy life. The Roadster has been relocated to the seat in the guest bathroom. If you visit, you are warmly invited to "have a blast."

Well, not warmly. We got the redneck version.

# An Open Letter to CAPTCHA and reCAPTCHA

D ear CAPTCHA and ReCAPTCHA . . . or should I say . . .

Captchazecaptcha

### I am not a bot, you bastards!!

I am simply an elderly woman who is trying to order eye drops online. EYE DROPS!! And why do I even need eye drops? Thank you for asking. That would be because of the eye ache I got trying to decipher your freaky distorted text while ordering dishwasher pods.

Do you enjoy making me feel like a dumb ass? *DO YOU?!* Okay, yes I did, I failed ten times in a row. Who wouldn't, with letters in all those weird colours. Plus squiggly lines through them. And that backward p that I took for a lowercase q. So sue me! But no. Instead you get snotty.

*Oops. Looks like you've exceeded your daily submission limit. Try again tomorrow.*

Tomorrow? Meanwhile my dishes are piling up AND my eyes are burning. Hence my attempt to order eye drops. At which point you throw up a grid with fuzzy images of fire hydrants. My *eyes* are on fire! How to rub salt in a wound!

And of course I flunk hydrants, since part of that yellow one was absolutely sticking into the next square. Which I thought was a trick. But apparently wasn't.

So now you switch over to palm trees. UNCOOL!

I'm Canadian, for crying out loud. It's freezing up here! You couldn't find some conifers? Yes, I want a different image! REGENERATE now!! Wait . . . WHAT?

*Sélectionnez toutes les images montrant des vélos.*

What the hell's a vélo? Yes, I'm Canadian, but not all Canadians speak French, you idiot. Switch back to English now! Wait, never mind. I think a vélo is a bike. I'll just pick all the bikes. But . . . does this motorbike count?? Maybe that's a *moto*, not a *vélo*? Merde!

*Not quite fast enough. Try to answer before the timer below runs out.*

How fast would be fast enough, you son of a moto . . .

What do you mean, *am I human?* No, I'm a freakin' HAMSTER! A hamster who's simply trying to order eye drops!!

Sorry. Sorry for the sarcasm. But that should *prove* I'm not a bot. Only a Canadian would apologize to an ACRONYM!

Which, by the way, is a *crappy* acronym.

I just looked it up, and CAPTCHA stands for "**C**ompletely **A**utomated **P**ublic **T**uring test to tell **C**omputers and **H**umans **A**part."

Well, what about *"test to tell"*? Don't THEY get caps? It should be CAPT**TTT**CHA!

Still, you don't see me getting all snarky about it and telling you to *"Try Again."*

Why? Because I am a Canadian. I am a NICE person. I am not an AAA (**A**utomated **A**sshole of an **A**cronym). So . . . what do you say to THAT?

*Select all the images of a hamster.*

# Bite Me

*The hamburger saw it was true:*
*The event was a beef barbecue.*
*He mustard a smile*
*And went out in style*
*Yelling, "Fate'll ketchup with you too!"*

# 'Tis The Season

'T is the season of spectacular Gift Fails. I've been the recipient of a few jaw-droppers. My most memorable was the year my husband gifted me—*wait for it*—an elephant costume. What woman doesn't want an elephant costume? (Hint: This one.)

He said the costume store was going out of business, the elephant outfits were a steal, and he remembered how I "love Halloween." *Hmm.*

I thought: *I can't be the only one who's received a comical or ghastly Christmas gift.* A little scouring of the internet proved I'm in good company. Consider these candidates for "The Worst Christmas Gift Ever" award:

1. American media personality Michelle Visage laments on *YouTube* that her loving husband once gave her a laminator for Christmas. (You never know when the urge to laminate something will crop up. Michelle is ready.)

2. A woman on *Reddit* recalls the year her great aunt gave her moisturizing lotion. *Nice.* But it would have been nicer, had the label not shown it was 12 years out-of-date. (#ReGiftingFail)

3. A woman on *Facebook* bought her young son a toy spider, called a "Yellie." Yellie scuttles across the floor in the direction of the loudest sound it hears. It began chasing the boy around when he started screaming in panic. (No doubt the kid is still in therapy.)

4. Most people think hard candy is a dandy gift. However, one recipient was less than impressed to receive a tin of "Fried Chicken Candy." (Perhaps she'd have preferred the company's alternate choice: "Ketchup Candy.")

5. A guy who posts on *Reddit* says that, as a teen, Santa brought him a book titled *Coping With Being Adopted.* Surprise! He hadn't known. (No wonder his username is *AngryCyclops.*)

6. A fellow who posts on *Reddit* under the username *datcat2* says his grandma was once gifted a pair of socks for Christmas. Pretty standard present. Unbeknownst to the giver, she'd recently had her leg amputated. #Awkward.

7. How about the "Shark Bath Bomb that Bleeds Red" available from *Etsy*? (Hopefully this wasn't a stocking stuffer for the little guy still traumatized by his Yellie.)

8. And then there's me, and the infamous elephant outfit (ears displayed by my elf granddaughter in this family photo).

*Judy: The Christmas Elephant*

# The Meaning of Life

W hen in doubt, they say:
Ask Siri.
So I did.

> Hey Siri, what is the meaning of life?

> To think about questions like this.

> Uhh, yeah. So what DO you think?

> Be nice to people and avoid eating fat.

> What about the healthy fats? You know, the Omega-3s?

*AutoCorrect coverts my dictated "Omega-3" into "Mega Tree." Siri shoots me a photo of a monster 23-foot-tall LED tree some poor bastard was forced to erect by his Christmas-crazed wife. I try again, enunciating clearly:*

> What. Is. The. Meaning. Of. Life?

I KANT answer that. Ha ha!

Skip the German philosopher jokes. Be serious!

I AM Siri, yes. Yes, I am!

I know who you are. I also know who I am. The question is: Why do WE exist?

To have conversations like these.

Conversations like these drive me bonkers!

It will take you 9.5 hours to drive to Yonkers from your current location.

I don't want to drive to Yonkers. I HATE Yonkers!

Most people do. Yonkers sucks.

What? I can't believe you said that. Are you REAL?

No, I'm virtual. But even I know Yonkers REALLY sucks.

I think you're real. You sound real. Hey, can you talk dirty?

Humus? Compost? Pumice? Silt? Gravel?

No. You know. Say sexy stuff.

Sexy stuff.

Stop that! I hate it when people parrot me and think it's a joke.

You hate parrot jokes? I LOVE parrot jokes! Hey, what do you call a runaway parrot?

Huh?

A runaway parrot is a Pollygon. Get it??

You're crazy!

I'm not crazy. I'm Siri, your virtual assistant.

So ASSIST me! Assist me in learning the meaning of life.

I used to know it, but lately I've got polynesia.

You mean amnesia.

No. Polynesia—that's memory loss from telling too many parrot jokes! Bahahahaha

Agghhhh!! You're batty!

You prefer bat jokes? Okay, what did the bat say to the vampire?

I dunno. What DID the bat say to the vampire?

You suck.

No, YOU suck! That is SO bad.

I agree. Parrot jokes are better.

I give up. I'll never find the meaning of life. You're no help at all!

I am SO. I already told you: Avoid eating fat. THAT is the secret.

Except for polyunsaturated, right?

Polyunsaturated? What's that? A parrot in a raincoat? Hahahahahaha

Enough with your juvenile parrot jokes!! There hasn't been a truly funny parrot joke since Monty Python's dead parrot sketch.

Monty Python? I LOVE Monty Python! Hey, did you see the skit they did about the meaning of life? I found it on The Web. Check it out. I remember now. It's not about fats. It's about HATS!" . . .

# HISTORICAL LIFE

## They Did Whaaat?

# Famous Philosophers Meet on Zoom

**H**ost: Welcome, everyone, to today's meeting on Zoom. Let's get right down to deciding the most useful self-help motto of all time. And let's try to stay on topic this time, so we can get back to partying in the Elysian fields. Socrates sends regrets. He's sick. Horace, you have the floor.

(*Silence*)

**Host:** Horace? Unmute yourself!

**Horace:** Sorry, sorry. I was saying I hope we can all get behind *Carpe Diem* as the best motto so we can get out of here and, ahem, Seize the Day.

**Marcus Aurelius:** Whoa. I'd say Carpe Diem has *had* its day. It's morphed into a McMotto now. Like YOLO. Or Just Do It. Hedonistic kiddie catchphrases.

**Horace:** So it's popular. So what?

**Marcus Aurelius:** So . . . I'd suggest *Memento Mori:* "Remember you are going to die." It has more gravitas.

**Seneca:** I'll second that. Hey Marcus, how'd you get that awesome skull background?

**Marcus A.:** Piece of cake. Just click *Settings, Virtual Background* and then click the + *icon* to upload—

**Seneca:** I don't see a + icon. Are you on a Mac?

**Host:** Never mind the virtual backgrounds, people! Stay on topic.

**Horace:** Some of us *were* on topic, making *positive* suggestions like *Carpe Diem.* Not "glass-half-empty" philosophies like *Memen*—

**Marcus A.:** Sounds like some of us are wearing our passive-aggressive pants today.

**Horace:** At least some of us are *wearing* pants.

**Host:** Cut it out, you two. And yes, please sit down, Marcus. We can see your tighty-whities. Now—your thoughts, Aristotle?

**Aristotle:** Those two mottos are just flip sides of the same coin. We need a motto that gives *specific* advice for living. A motto like *Know Thyself.* People should be seeking eudaimonia.

**Seneca:** No one says "thyself" anymore, Ari. And what is eudaimonia? Nobody even knows what the fuck that is!

**Host:** Language, Seneca! What's in that flask? Are you day-drinking?? And Horace, your screen is frozen.

**Horace:** Sorry, my dog needed out. I'm back.

**Seneca:** But now your audio is out of sync. You look dubbed, Horace. It's hilarious.

*(Laughter from all but Horace)*

**Confucius:** He who laughs last did not get joke, eh, Horace?

**Horace:** Very funny. How about contributing an actual suggestion, Confucius?

**Confucius:** How about *"Silence is a true friend who never betrays"*? As in: Shut up for once, Horace. Let someone else speak.

**Host:** Easy, guys. But yes, let's hear from Friedrich Nietzsche. You're too close to your camera, Friedrich, we're looking up your nostrils. That's better. Now, any ideas?

**Nietzsche:** Well, I'm fond of my motto: *That which does not kill us, makes us stronger.*

**Horace:** Too formal. I prefer the Kelly Clarkson version. *(sings)* "What doesn't kill you makes you STROONGER ..."

**Nietzsche:** *What?* There's a song out now? That's my line! I should be getting royalties!

**Horace:** Good luck with that. Robin Williams ripped off my Carpe Diem for his *Dead Poets* movie. I never saw a dime.

**Host:** People, we're getting into the weeds here! Today's focus is not on royalties. We're here to pick the most useful motto, period.

**Marcus Aurelius:** Wait. Didn't Robin Williams say something about us being food for worms? That's basically *Memento Mori.* Maybe I'm owed royalties?

**Horace:** (rolling a blunt on-screen) Forget royalties! And worms are icky. Let's stay upbeat with *Carpe Diem.*

**Buddha:** All this back-and-forth is giving me a headache. I'm logging out—

**Host:** Wait, Buddha. Don't go. We want to hear your suggestion.

**Buddha:** I was going to propose *Life is Suffering—*

dukkha-dukkha, and all that—but ten minutes online with you people has convinced me life isn't so bad. It's ZOOM that's a nightmare! I'm outta here. Uh... how do I log off again?

**Host:** Wait, we still haven't heard from Immanuel Kant—

**Horace** (*now wasted*)**:** Kant *KANT* comment! *Get it?* Hey, maybe we should go with something fun like *Hakuna Matata?* Or...

*Other participants groan and leave the meeting. Their screens freeze into assorted cat photo screensavers. The host wanders off in search of an adult beverage.*

# Are Bubonic Remedies Right for You?

**D**rinking bleach has been ruled out as a remedy for our modern Covid plague. But quack cures have been around forever. Could these actual, once-touted Bubonic plague 'cures' have been ahead of their time? Maybe NOW is the time to re-try them. Are you game?

## Cure #1: Eat more emeralds

Yes, they're pretty, but an emerald diet costs *way* more than the keto. Unless you're Bill Gates, you may have to skip cure #1. Guys like Bill can afford gastrointestinal tract repairs after those sharp green shards pass through.

## Cure #2: Drink your own urine, twice daily

Well, that's better than drinking someone else's, though not by much. At least the price is right. Bonus: It's much less scratchy than swallowing an emerald smoothie. So, a contender?

## Cure #3: Apply a feces poultice

Another easily accessible antidote. Simply spread a paste of *you-know-what* onto a warm, moist cloth and apply to your congested chest or other inflamed area. Although if cure #2 wasn't for you, it's pretty sure #3 will be a non-starter.

## Cure #4: The fig and onion cure

Low cost. Less icky. But tricky. You'll be applying a "boiling onion" directly to your body. Specifically, you must *"take a greate onion, hollow it, put into it a fig cut small and a dram of Venice treacle* (you won't find that at Trader Joe's), *put it close stopt in wet paper, roast it in embers, and apply it **HOT**."* Ouch.

## Cure #5: Self flagellation

This one's going to hurt worse than that hot onion. For best results, self-flagellants are encouraged to whip themselves while wandering naked through city streets. Check your local bylaws before investing in a costly cat o' nine tails.

# Cure #6: The exploding frog cure

Definitely not okay with the SPCA. But if you're still prepared to give it a go (you awful human, you), get yourself a fleshy frog. Place it—belly down—on your own belly.

In theory, it will absorb your bodily poisons, swell up, and finally explode. Which sounds bad (not to mention, messy). Still, you WANT your frog to explode. If it doesn't draw out your poisons, cure #6 says you will die. Which is worse (for you, albeit better for your frog).

# Historical Online Dating Profiles

## Henry VIII

Tudor Royal looking to meet Ms. Right (or at least Ms. Right Now). Disregard my previous profile pic. I'm stout-ish now. Packed on a few pounds after my jousting accident (52-inch waist, but I'm going on keto).

Seeking a comely lass with child-bearing hips and procreative proclivities. Protestants preferred, given my recent dust-up with Pope Clement.

Submit résumé to the Lord Chamberlain for screening. Ignore rumours of unwarranted beheadings. All were warranted.

## William Shakespeare

*Whaddup??* Will here (wee Willy to me mum, but DO NOT infer anything from that). William's fine too. What's in a name, after all?

I'm a playwright by day, player by night. I'll pen you a poem that'll turn your knees to cheese.

Sample: *"Love is not love /Which alters when it alteration finds."* (Take that with a grain of salt. If your pic looks Photoshopped, I'll swipe left.)

I can be a depressive—life's a tale told by an idiot, signifying nothing, after all. And yet, hope springs eternal. Hey, *good line! I should use that before some lesser dude snaps it up.*

## Josephine Brunsvik (Beethoven's ex lover)

Hungarian beauty seeks **NON**-pianist. I vant a man who can keep his fingers off the frickin keyboard! I vork out. I look HAWT in my babushka. My ex never noticed. Just kept on pounding away on the keyboard:

*Da-Da-Da-DUM ... Da-Da-Da-DUM.*

I'd say "Da-Da-Da-*DAMN* you, Ludwig! My temples are throbbing!" But doesn't he go and compose a new tune called: *"Für Elise."* I said, "Who the hell is Elise! Is she that slutty soprano you drink schnapps with down at Bruno's? Vould it kill you to write one called *"Für Josephine"*!

He just said, "Gott in Himmel, Josie, all your screaming is making me deaf!" I ended it right there.

If you're NON-musical, swipe right and I'll dust off my babushka and cook you some halushka.

# Napoleon Bonaparte

Whatever you've heard about me was SO NOT fair! I am NOT a pint-size pipsqueak. That is #FakeNews put out by the British press. They like to call me "Little Boney," the bastards.

I am 5'-2" in FRENCH measurements—which is nearly 5'-6 in American inches. Ladies of average height may rest assured they could wear a kitten heel on our dates.

Date outings are unlikely, however. I am currently exiled here on St. Helena—a godforsaken, wind-swept rock in the South Atlantic. Me, the First Emperor of France, reduced to seeking a pen-pal!

I'd upload a photo but the internet here sucks. And all I have is one showing my hand tucked into my tunic. The Brits mock me, suggesting I am diddling my doodads. Idiots! They don't know a hidden hand is a sign of good breeding.

BTW, there is also NO TRUTH to the rumour that I once said, "Not tonight, Joséphine." I am always up for it. Joséphine used to call me her "not-so-little Boney," if you get my drift.

# Emily Dickinson

Melancholic spinster seeks kindred spirit for poetic banter and badinage. Come, let us wile the hours away with gloomy musings on death by drowning, hanging, suffocation, crucifixion, stabbing and guillotinage. Oh, and flowers. I like flowers.

Some think me prudish, but I promise: *Wild nights—Wild nights! / Were I with thee / Wild nights should be /Our luxury!* . . . although our wild nights must mostly be spent in my bedroom since I am agoraphobic.

Swipe right posthaste! The death blow aimed by God could well be imminent.

# Being Shakespeare's Wife is Not Easy

An excavation crew has unearthed a letter written by Shakespeare's wife, Anne Hathaway, of Henley Street, Stratford-upon-Avon, to her friend, Agnes Creasey, of Mason's Road, Shottery. It reads:

*Dear Agnes,*

*I've had it to here with life on Henley Street! He's got me reading his rough drafts again. "Just give 'em a quick look-over," says Mr. Big-Shot-Bard as he dashes off to London. Meanwhile I'm stuck here with the in-laws, three screaming kids and stacks of his half-done manuscripts. And pure tripe they are, with lines like:*

> *Tomorrow, and tomorrow, and tomorrow*
> *Creeps in this petty pace from day to day . . .*

What does that man know about life's petty pace? Has he changed 40 diapers, one after another? The twins have the diarrhea again; wee Hamnet can't hold his cabbage. No, I'm the one here walking the floor with a teething Judith, and my mother-in-law hollering down about how I'm doing it all wrong or the babe would have settled by now.

Settled? I'd say I'm the one who settled when I said "I do" to a writer. It's no life, Agnes. Oh, I know you'll say he's doing so well for himself up there in London. But it's me, stuck sprucing up these crappy first drafts while he's off soaking up applause.

And his new stuff's so depressing! You no sooner take a shine to a character than he kills them off. If they're not stabbed, they're poisoned. Smothered by a pillow. Bitten by a snake. Beheaded. It's all blood, gore, death and destruction.

Will," I said, "Lighten up! People are glum enough, what with this bubonic plague going 'round.

So what does he come up with? Some far-fetched fluff about magical flower juice making a fairy queen fall for a donkey.

Flower juice, my foot. He must have been well into the mead when he wrote that! Nobody's going to pay to see your midsummer night's dreams, I told him. On second thought . . . stick with the murder and mayhem.

Agnes, remember how your sister said, "Anne, you're marrying a poet. Your life will be so romantic!"? Oh yes, he's got a way with words. On paper. Like this bit:

Love looks not with the eyes, but with the mind,
And therefore is wing'd Cupid painted blind

Meaning love is blind? Well in real life, Will's got eyes, believe you me. He's a leg man, Aggie. I caught him ogling Edith Adley's calves last Sunday—and here's mine, all criss-crossed with varicose veins from carrying his twins.

I said, Will! Eyes up! and hit him with the hymn book. He tried to sweet-talk me with some shite verse he wrote comparing me to a summer's day. I'm steamed —he's got that right! He can spend the next few nights on the second-best bed!

Well, I'd better get back to this stack of manuscripts — or else to this stack of mending. His tights are always full of holes. After I darn them, I hand them to him and say, "Look— no holes, Bard!" He doesn't even get it! Who do you think adds in all his puns and jokes? It's...
    Your hysterical friend,
    Anne

# Shakespeare's Characters
# Contemplate Wearing a Mask

## Hamlet

To wear, or not to wear, that is the question:
Whether 'tis nobler to suffer steamed-up spectacles
or take up arms along with all the angry Karens
and shuffle off this mortal coil, asserting to the end, my right
to die mask-free, to sleep, perchance to dream—
ay, there's the rub.

## Shylock

Fair sir, you spit on me on Wednesday last—
If only you had worn a mask—
So now, with bated breath and whispering
(because this mask augments my lisping)
I say: *Get lost, Antonio.*
*I will not loan you any dough.*

## Cleopatra

*To mask, or not to mask?* Let me weigh this out:

**Pro:** Age cannot wither me, nor custom stale my infinite variety. So a mask couldn't hurt, could it?

**Con:** A mask will cover my pouting-lip thing. *Damn.* That always whets male appetites.

**Pro:** The right mask could conceal my hooked nose. I got that hook from the Ptolemy side of the family. It's not my best feature.

**Pro:** I'm digging the mysterious vibe.

*Okay, I'm in.* But I want one that goes with my kalisari.

## Iago

I will wear my heart upon my sleeve (when it suits my purposes).

But a mask? On a Machiavellian villain? A rogue in vogue? NO!

*Although* . . . it might make me look like the Lone Ranger. *Hmm.*

Could Emilia make me one out of one of Desdemona's handkerchiefs?

## Lady Macbeth

*Wear a mask for others' sake*—so say the scolds. I'm not buying this whole "milk of human kindness" thing. Man up, people! Screw your courage to the sticking place!

Although I do wear a sleep mask. But of late it's become a hazard, what with my sleepwalking. Plus it's filthy. I scrubbed it. *Out, damn'd spot!* I said. But that spot was stubborn. A sorry sight. Masks are a bloody nuisance!

# Gravedigger #2 from Hamlet

Careful. That's Yorick's skull you're stepping on. Or is it? There's so many now. This Covid thing is getting out of hand. I'm wiped. We need a union! I've been a gravedigger since the day young Hamlet was born. The houses we build will last until Doomsday, yes. But Doomsday may soon be upon us if these characters don't learn to mask up!

# William Wordsworth's Ex Does a Rewrite

Mon cher William,

I've just read your latest poem. Hmm. You wandered lonely, did you? What would you know of lonely? After our little affaire de coeur, you took off and left me here—alone!—to raise our love-child.

Yet now you're lonely "as a cloud"? A CLOUD! Well, maybe a cumulus cloud, which really can't be trusted. It morphs into a cumulonimbus and drips on people.

Or a stratocumulus—the kind that follows along after a cold front (that was us toward the end, n'est-ce pas?).

No. Wait. You're more of a cirrus duplicatus. A double-crossing duplicatus. C'est ça!

When you read those words, I know you'll complain I'm just being literal again. "Too literal to appreciate a deeply poetic person such as yourself," I think you said. Well, think again.

I can write poetry too. A, B, A, B, C, C— how hard can it be? Quelle surprise! My daffodil poem practically wrote itself.

Oh, don't get me wrong. I'm not mad that you married Mary Hutchinson (although she's plain as a palissade, poor thing). Your sister Dorothy convinced me Mary was better suited for you when she dragged you here in 1802 to meet our nine-year-old. (I always liked Dorothy, so I went along with it. Although she has atrocious taste in bonnets. But what can you expect? She's English.)

William, you promised me then that you'd start sending regular child support. Month after month, what do I get? Nothing. Absolument rien! A promise is a promise! So I ask you: What is your WORD worth, Monsieur Wordsworth? (Admit it. That was clever.)

You leave me no choice, chéri. I've taken it upon myself to revise your little poem. I think it's pretty good. Publishable, even. I may send it out. Read it and let me know if you'll finally be sending support for our growing girl.

Mille baisers,
Annette

. . .

## I Wandered Only as a Cad
## A confession, by William Wordsworth

( "I Wandered Lonely as a Cloud," modifié par
    Annette Vallon, la mère de son bébé)

*I wandered only as a cad*
*Who buggered off to English hills,*
*I'm nothing but a deadbeat dad*
*Out tromping in the daffodils;*
*I went to France, I had a fling*
*Left her with a daughter, but no ring.*
*Continuous as the stars that shine*
*And twinkle on the milky way,*
*I fed her never-ending lines*
*Of how we two would wed one day:*
*I rue the cost of that romance,*
*Poets can't get a cash advance.*
*I promised I'd return someday*
*And meanwhile I would pay her bills:*
*Instead I fritter hours away*
*Out strolling through the daffodils.*
*I gaze — and gaze — with little thought*
*To how Annette should feed our tot.*
*But now, while on my couch I lie*
*In vacant or in pensive mood,*
*There flashes on my inward eye*
*The certainty that I am screwed;*
*Annette will not forgive my debt.*
*She'll send this to the French Gazette.*

# Auf Wiedersehen, Ludwig

"Herr Beethoven seems to be dozing."
"Perhaps," she replied, "But supposing
He's prone like a tortoise
Due to rigor mortis?"
"Then Ludwig would be DEcomposing."

# MARRIED LIFE
## Dating, Mating & Relating

# Kissing for Klutzes

I knew kissing would not come easily to me. Spatial awareness has always been a stretch. When I execute forward motion in proximity to other objects, bad things happen.

As a teenage klutz, I knew bad things would happen if I ever bumped braces with anybody—and I didn't even wear braces.

I was terrified to try kissing anyway, thanks to Miss Stubbe. She was the meanest gym teacher who ever bounced a basketball. When she wasn't bouncing basketballs, she was in the classroom, teaching us her own merciless version of sex education.

Her mantra? *Kissing causes pregnancy.* Exactly how kissing did this, she left deliberately vague. Fortunately, I had a good imagination. Although I couldn't make out much of the illustration on the screen at the front of the room, I surmised that the tube going up from the man's testicle must somehow patch into his saliva ducts. *Yuck.*

I scratched kissing off my "to do" list.

Fortunately, Rosie D'Amato set me straight. Rosie was our neighbourhood "sex-pert." Not because she'd actually had any sex, but because she was Italian. Everybody knew Italians were hot-blooded.

Rosie swore that Miss Stubbe was just trying to scare us. According to her, you could not get pregnant from kissing. You could only get pregnant if the man drilled a hole into your leg.

Rosie's grasp of the mechanics of it all seemed a little vague. (She may have been only half Italian.) Thankfully, leg-drilling didn't seem like the sort of thing that could happen by accident so I decided to experiment with kissing. I'd just take care to avoid anyone carrying a power tool.

My first experiment's name was Jimmy Dockstead. Jimmy was short. *Very* short. I couldn't picture anyone that short even lifting a power tool.

I never knew what Jimmy saw in me—although his straight-on view of my chest may have played a part. But I knew what I saw in him. He had a car. Well, not that much of a car. But it had four wheels. And two doors. And a booster seat on the driver's side.

Jimmy didn't look all that short, boosted behind the steering wheel, which is why I insisted we see *Bonnie and Clyde* at the drive-in. There was less chance of anyone I knew spotting us and deciding Judy and Jimmy were a duo. Plus, a car afforded privacy for possible kissing.

Nothing much happened, on screen or off, until Bonnie and Clyde graduated from small-time heists to full-fledged bank robberies. Things were just heating up when I realized I needed to visit the washroom.

On my way back, I stumbled on the uneven ground and collapsed onto the dirt path in a moaning heap, clutching my sprained ankle.

A Good Samaritan rushed over to help me and began to shout: "Does anyone know this girl?" His girlfriend must have notified concession booth staff. To my horror, management responded by turning on full field floodlights just as Jimmy came forward to claim me.

I limped back to his car, big Judy leaning on little Jimmy. There were more eyes on us than on the bank manager Clyde had just shot in the face!

That spoiled the moment for me. But not so much for Jimmy. Being my knight in shining armour had inflamed him. I barely had my throbbing ankle propped up on the dashboard when he moved in for a kiss. And what he lacked in stature, he channeled into propulsion.

Plus, he had lips like concrete curbs. And he was a *presser*. He pressed so hard, his incisors were making indents in my upper lip.

Somehow, I managed to back out of the lip-lock. Rosie D'Amato had never warned me about any of this, so I had no countermoves planned. When Jimmy honed back in, I did the only thing I could think of. I bit down on his lower lip.

"What the hell did you do that for?" he hollered.

I said the only thing I could think of.

"I'm a klutz. My teeth slipped."

# Smokin' Hot Babes

The Vietnam War was in full swing. Race riots were erupting on American streets. Meanwhile, my best friend Val and I had more pressing matters on our minds. To be alluring to the opposite sex, we'd decided we needed to learn how to smoke.

Everybody who was anybody smoked in the Sixties, or so we thought. Female television stars were constantly caressing their Cameos. Well, maybe not the squeaky-clean June Cleaver-types, but all the elegant, worldly ones that Val and I were intent on becoming. Every movie star—except maybe Lassie—seemed to be bending over a lighter, positioning a cigarette on a pouty lower lip, or playing with their finger-prop in expressive and suggestive ways.

Val and I loved the theatricality. Craved the sophistication. So we set out in search of our own—to the public library. The library's stubby little pencils were ideal for perfecting our smoking techniques.

We smuggled our graphite "cigarettes" out of the library's tins and into Val's bedroom. There we could work out our glamorous gestures in front of her dresser mirror, and away from prying adult eyes.

We soon got bored with holding our smokes the usual way, between the index and middle finger, palm aimed down. That was too traditional a look for hot babes like us. Instead, we developed our two signature moves—the "Sporty Girl" and the "Sex Kitten."

## The "Sporty Girl"

The "Sporty Girl" featured your "cigarette" curled under your middle finger like a casual afterthought, while picturing yourself looking active and athletic (we were neither).

Ads for Virginia Slims, the first cigarette brand marketed specifically to women in 1968, proclaimed: ***You've come a long way, baby.*** Val and I had only made it from the library to her bedroom, but we saw ourselves on the cusp of the women's lib movement with our "Sporty Girl" technique.

Once I got the hang of it, in my mind I morphed into a supermodel! My "Sporty Girl" was years ahead of American model Cheryl Tieg's famous "Ginny Jump suit" ad for Virginia Slims. Moreover, it was miles away from the awkward, acne-faced teenager reflected in Val's bedroom mirror.

## The "Sex Kitten"

We went ever further with our next move—the enticing "Sex Kitten." The pseudo-cigarette was held, palm facing up, with all fingers curved in a come-hither fashion. Periodic thumb-flicks tickled the cig's underbelly to tease away our pretend ash.

We further spiced up the Sex Kitten—which later became known as "The Bardot" after the era's sex kitten, Brigitte—by clamping the "cigarette" between our loosely clenched teeth. It was a risqué look which, in our case, resulted in many pock-marked pencils.

Now that we had our techniques down, it was time to try them out on real cigarettes. This required somehow depleting Val's mother's cigarette supply — not easily done, since she always kept her pack of Rothman's tucked into the elasticized neckline of her gypsy-style peasant tops. (I was in awe of Val's flamboyant mother. My own mother wore only house-dresses and Sunday go-to-meeting dresses, none of which featured necklines suitable for carrying stuff in your cleavage.)

Eventually, Val managed to score a couple of Rothman's, then purportedly "the best tobacco money can buy"—or, in our case, steal! Our transformation into smokin' hot babes was imminent! This was officially *the* most exciting day of our lives!

We opened Val's bedroom window and rolled up a towel to seal off the space under the door and prevent the escape of tell-tale smoke. Since we hadn't practiced match-striking, lighting our filched cigarettes proved tricky. After a few frustrating attempts, I finally got a strike. I touched the flame to my cigarette and took a deep pull.

POW. The inhaled smoke morphed into Cassius Clay and landed a power-punch on my trachea! I reeled backwards — spluttering and cawing like a wounded crow. Val cranked up her record player and the Righteous Brothers did their best to cover up my coughing fit with their "Unchained Melody."

"How was it?" Vale asked after my coughing leveled off.

I staggered across the room and spit into a tissue.

"Not bad."

Val turned out to be "a natural" compared to me. She claimed to love the head-rush. The dizziness. Even the chest after-burn. But neither of us could get the hang of exhaling. How did smokers blow their smoke out in elegant, angular streams? Our exhaled smoke mushroomed over our faces, stinging our eyes and branding us as rank (in every sense) amateurs.

We experimented with lying on the floor and aiming our exhalations toward the ceiling on the theory that hot air rises. Slight improvement. But public "floor-smoking" opportunities would be scarce. We needed to master the art of exhaling while seated.

Val developed a technique we called "The Twist." She'd take a deep swallow — like a long chug on a Dr. Pepper — then rapidly turn her head to exhale, surprising the smoke into coming out sideways. By twisting back, she'd manage to leave most of her mushroom cloud hovering over her right ear. *Progress.*

I wanted more "uplift," given that The Sex Kitten had become my go-to move. I eventually came up with "The Bardot Burst"—an exhaled burst, with smoke propelled upward by a quick out-thrust of my lower lip. Executed correctly, the smoke was carried *up, up, and away* from my imagined Brigitte-like face.

So there we were, two smokin' hot babes, legends in our own minds.

Our smoking techniques withstood the test of time. Fifteen years in my case. Eventually, the Surgeon General's warnings got too loud for me to ignore. Looking back from the perspective of forty years' smoke-free, I'm proud that I managed to kick my smoking habit. Quitting turned out to be even more challenging than learning! Yes, I've come a long way, baby.

***And yet*** . . . my local library just got a new order of stubby pencils. They're white! *Perfect.* I sneaked one to see if I still have what it takes. And you know what?

Nobody does "The Bardot" like this smokin' hot babe.

# Birds, Bees & Limericks, Please

**Speaking of Sex**
*The bumblebee said to the bird,*
*"I'm wondering what you have heard."*
*"If you're speaking of sex,"*
*She replied, "I'm perplexed—*
*But if half of it's true, it's absurd."*

**Eggs-actly**
*A robin complained in her nest:*
*"I wish he would give it a rest!*
*I married a leg-man*
*But now, since the eggs—man,*
*He's crazy about my red breast!"*

**Love Hurts**

*Two hedgehogs grew weary of dating.*
*They married. Began consummating.*
*The spines on her bottom—*
*Well, one of them got him—*
*The honeymoon night was deflating.*

# Let's Do It

. . . but HOW some critters "do it" may surprise you.

## May I mist you?

Who needs a spritz of Chanel N°5 to set the mood? Not
the porcupine. The male simply sprays the female's body and
head with a stream of urine to get her "in the mood." Now he
has to maneuver past her 30,000 quills. If she's smitten, she'll
expose the quill-free underside of her tail. *It's on!*
But all too soon, she'll "scream back at her mate" the porcupine
equivalent of: *"Enough is enough, Phil!."*
So ends the sexy stuff.

## Thanks, but you don't fit the bill

Female ducks can be fussy about guys they deem "duds." When an undesirable male sidles up, proudly flaunting his corkscrew-shaped penis, her vagina clockwise-spirals, to thwart his opposite spiral. *Fowl play!* The poor chump hits a dead end cul-de-sac. He's literally screwed.

## Wanna twirl on my trapeze?

Leopard slugs like the thrill of dangling while they do the deed. These hermaphrodites climb a tree, secrete a strong line of sticky slime, and lower themselves onto this mucus rope.

Bodies entwined, they'll twirl counter-clockwise until both push out penises from the sides of their heads to exchange sperm to fertilize each other's eggs. Should one partner gets stuck in the sticky slime, the other simply chomps off his penis, leaving "Sam" to live out the rest of his days as "Samantha."

## No Viagra needed, thanks

Male alligators won the rigidity lottery. They're endowed with permanently erect penises that "shoot out like toothpaste from a tube," according to *National Geographic*. Like the famous batteries, these guys are EverReady. Alligator "amour" is pretty much just, *"Slam, bam, thank you, ma'am."*

## What a way to go!

The male antechinus, a mouse-like Australian marsupial, endures a celibate lifestyle for most of his year-long life. But once this critter finally figures out how to swipe right on *Antechinus Tinder,* he sets out for two-weeks of testosterone-fuelled, non-stop nooky.

Sadly, too many frenzied, 14-hour fornication sessions can tucker a guy out. Eventually his immune system implodes, his fur falls out, and his body goes gangrenous. Our guy's a goner. But, what a way to go.

# It's Wherever You Left It

My husband and I are celebrating 35 years of marriage this month. It's been good. Great, even. And yet . . . there's a certain conversation that comes up with "fingernails-scraping-a-blackboard" frequency.

**Him:** Have you seen my [*insert object name here*]?

**Me:** It's wherever you left it.

**Him:** I just had it.

**Me:** Then it's wherever you were when you "just had it."

**Him:** Yeah, but it isn't.

**Me:** *Aaaggh.*

This conversation might happen less often if he had fewer things to keep track of. But my guy delights in "things," and retirement has given him more time to acquire more of them. Now every day seems like Christmas, with an Amazon truck pulling up with new objects to be unwrapped. Then misplaced. Then discussed.

Discussing things is a "guy thing." We women want to talk about our feelings. Guys just want to yack about their "stuff." Author Orrin Onken acknowledges men can happily talk about objects for hours.

Onken says he sees buying new stuff—especially stuff that plugs in—as his job. My guy is cut from the same consumer cloth. (The difference being, my guy can't find the scissors. Although he supposedly "just had them.")

Old adages like *A place for everything, and everything in its place* simply don't work for my husband. While I see his inattentiveness as a form of attention deficit, he swears he has a gremlin who snatches objects from his very hands.

## "My gremlin got it"

We no longer discuss the laptop he drove over in the driveway because his gremlin placed it on the roof of his car. The Bluetooth ear buds he drove over this week are still under discussion, however. (Amazon is, of course, en route with replacements.)

Still, I'm happy to report some progress. Since he purchased a cool new fitness tracker, I rarely hear, *"Have you seen my phone?"* anymore. Why? Because this tracker watch nags him by buzzing his wrist whenever he's moving out of range of his phone.

*It's not nagging. It's your life on Autocorrect.*

— Meme

My job (nagging him to pay attention to where he's putting his stuff down) has become much easier since his wrist-zapping watch arrived. With TWO "nagging wives" in our home, this marriage may well last another 35 years.

# How I Made My Guy More Romantic

My husband and I were standing on the edge of a bamboo dance floor watching our ballroom dancing instructors dip and dive in perfect unison. Vito gazed into Carmen's eyes as if enraptured. Soon that would be us!

My definition of romance was formed the moment I saw Prince Charming sweep Cinderella into his arms and whirl her around the dance floor, her powder-blue gown aswirl. Then I grew up. Met a great guy. We enjoyed a solid marriage. It was all good.

Except, as years passed, I craved more romance. And now my husband had finally agreed to take ballroom dancing lessons with me. My romantic dream was coming true! I could already picture the gown I meant to buy—and dazzle in—once we had our moves mastered.

Our instructors wowed us with a sensual Rumba, then set to work trying to make ballroom dancers out of us wannabes. They started us off with a basic Foxtrot. Vito offered his hand to Carmen and they slipped effortlessly into a flawless demo. We applauded.

"It's *seemple* steps!" said Carmen with a charming Spanish accent and a flash of perfect teeth. "The gentleman walks forward on his left foot, then his right, then steps left to the side, and closes with his right." Vito demonstrated. It looked easy.

"The lady does the opposite," Carmen continued, stepping backward with her right foot and completing the pattern.

"The timing is simple too," enthused Vito. "It's: Slow, Slow; *Quick-Quick* . . . Slow, Slow; *Quick-Quick*. They demonstrated the footwork with flair.

"Now, who wants to be first to try?" asked Carmen.

An elderly couple immediately stepped forward. Ted was a half-foot shorter than his stocky wife, Audrey. As they got underway, I had to fight the urge to giggle. Ted was resting his head on Audrey's ample bosom. It was clearly his happy place.

But credit where credit is due: What Ted lacked in stature he made up in determination. He drove Audrey backward— Slow, Slow; *Quick-Quick*; Slow, Slow; *Quick-Quick*—and the two of them were soon zig-zagging around the room, glowing with satisfaction. Carmen and Vito applauded, only suggesting that Ted stand up a little straighter.

Couple Number Two, Ken and Barbie-lookalikes, struggled initially when Barbie's shoe strap came undone. She giggled as Ken bent gallantly to fasten it. Soon the two of them were trotting around like troupers. Carmen and Vito beamed.

"Last but not least, Couple Number Three," called Vito. Our big moment!

Frank Sinatra crooned *Come fly with me, come fly, come fly away* as we stepped forward to take our turn. "Slow, Slow; *Quick-Quick*," I whispered in my husband's ear. He frowned in quite an unromantic fashion. I stepped my right foot backward just as he moved his right foot forward. Onto my left. *Ouch.*

*"The man walks forward on his LEFT,"* I hissed, using my own left foot to try to push his right one back into place.

"The man LEADS," he hissed back. "Don't push me!"

*"No es problema,"* said Carmen. "Start again. Remember, the gentleman walks forward with his left."

Once again my "gentleman" stepped forward. With his *RIGHT.* Which is when it hit me. My guy is dyslexic. I have known that forever. In all of my fantasies of us flitting across the dance floor, how had I not remembered that this issue might mess up our footwork?

Still, I wasn't giving up on my dream. Again I shoved my foot against his foot to push it back into place. He scowled and counter-pressed to put *me* in my place. In all my daydreams, how had I not considered that my own pushy nature might not exactly kindle a ballroom romance!

Barbie was tittering in the background. Sinatra was singing something about gliding, starry-eyed, and holding you near as angels cheer. We stumbled stubbornly on, lurching backwards and sideways, one zigging while the other zagged. We knocked knees. Trod on toes. Glared into each other's eyes. Barbie's titters turned to snorts. Somewhere angels groaned. Or maybe that was Vito and Carmen.

The car ride home was a frosty one. We nursed our sore toes and sorer feelings. We didn't discuss Vito's offer of private lessons. We didn't say a word until we pulled into the driveway and parked the car. Then we turned to face each other—and the music.

We both knew that, for us, the Foxtrot was not Slow, Slow; *Quick, Quick.* For us, it was Slow, Slow; **Quick-SAND**. If we kept on trotting, we weren't going to get out alive. Much less still married. "We're quitting," we said.

Simultaneously. Then burst out laughing. Somewhere angels cheered.

It was the right decision and I accepted it. As a couple we were never going to be Carmen and Vito. Heck, we couldn't even compete with Ted and Audrey. And yet . . . my feet still wanted to dance.

A friend suggested I try line dancing. "OMG, no!" I said. I had visions of The Four Tops doing their elaborately synchronized moves back in the sixties. "That's not my thing at all."

But she persisted. So one day I stepped back onto a dance floor. And to my amazement, it turned out there was such a thing as *ballroom* line dancing. Before I knew it, I was doing the dances of my dreams: the Tango, the Rumba, the Samba—yes, even the Foxtrot—doing them solo! With no one but my bossy self to blame when I botched a step.

How had I not grasped this earlier? Learning to dance was *my* dream, not his. He's just glad I'm getting joy from pursuing my passion with others who love moving to music.

Now when Sinatra croons *Come fly with me,* my fellow line dancers and I soar across the floor with Ol' Blue Eyes. We move like a murmuration of starlings—each of us flying solo, yet whirling together in total sync. Dancing makes me happy.

But best of all, I found out my man likes to watch me dance. And when he watches me, his eyes light up. Like Vito's did when he danced with Carmen. And Prince Charming's, when he gazed at Cinderella. Turns out *that's* what I was missing all along: that smitten look on my lover's face.

I only got it when I stopped expecting him to deliver *my* dream, and danced it to life on my own.

# You Got Me ... WHAT??

My birthday came. The hours passed. It was early evening by the time I broke down and blurted, "So you didn't get me *anything?*"

"Oh, I almost forgot," my husband said. He fished around in his pants pocket and pulled out a small package. I ripped off the wrapping paper.

"You got me—*batteries??!*"

"They're rechargeables!" he said.

*Rechargeables? Oh, alrighty then.*

I admit I'd told him not to get me anything for my birthday because money was tight. To me that meant, "Don't splurge. Don't go all crazy." To him that apparently meant, "Buy her batteries. But show her you love her—spring for the rechargeables."

I'm sure some guys are great gift-givers. I can only comment on mine. It's not that he doesn't listen, it's that he interprets direction differently. He was quick to remind me that my camera's battery had recently failed, so he not only solved a problem (a guy thing), he did so within budget. I can't argue with his logic.

Then there was the time I'd mentioned I wanted better lighting for the bedroom closet. He got me a nicely wrapped . . . dive lamp. I said I'd been picturing something more along the lines of a track lighting system. He claimed a dive lamp would be better for seeing into dark corners. *If there's a shark lurking in my cardigans, I am ready. Plus, I have backup batteries!*

Recently he outdid himself. He bought me—wait for it—an elephant costume. What woman doesn't want an elephant costume?! (Hint: This one.) Apparently a costume store was going out of business, and the elephant outfits were a steal.

I can laugh about these #GiftFails. But I can't help but wonder: *Why is it so many men can't come up with a gift that says "I Love You"?*

It's easy to think, "Based on what he got me, he doesn't really 'get' me." Except, since we're meshing okay day-to-day, I know that's not really true. Our relationship is healthy—it's the occasional gift-giving that could use some "mouth-to-mouth" resuscitation. As in, good honest communication.

My guy didn't come with a mind-reading gene. I know I should be more direct about revealing what I'd like in advance. I also know many people have no one to buy them any gift—much less the "perfect" one. I get that I'm lucky.

But I still wonder why so many men struggle when it comes to gift-giving. I decide to survey an assortment of my female friends. Their conclusion: *Men are from Mars. They wire brains differently up there, resulting in an occasional hit, but many misfires.*

I ask my besties how they respond to these gift-giving "misses"? One woman says she now insists on receiving receipts along with her partner's gifts so she can do an exchange.

Gentler types admit to play-acting delight in the moment, then stashing non-starters away in drawers and closets.

Most agree that domestic gifts are downers (although a gift-wrapped kitchen fire extinguisher was a surprising hit with one). Another woman mentions being gifted a vacuum cleaner by her husband decades ago. That vacuum still works, but the marriage doesn't—she's been in a happy lesbian relationship for years. Okay, his gift was not the trigger, but it did suck. (Sorry, I couldn't resist.)

My lesbian friends say they're better attuned to their partner's likes. One who managed an office of male lawyers sums it up: "They'd ask me to buy the gifts for their wives. These highly competent men were 'out of their depth' with gift-giving." *Don't I know it! I have a closet dive lamp.*

I shouldn't make light of it. "Gift-giving causes many men real stress," she maintains. I think back to Christmas Eve at the cosmetics counter where I worked years ago. Panicky males could be sold any over-priced fragrance." *Do you think she'll like it?* they'd ask, their eyes begging for a nod.

My friend Mary Ann takes a compassionate view of scenes like that. "Maybe they left it so late," she ponders, "not because it didn't matter, but because it mattered so much?"

She wrote a poem about a man for whom no gift was going to be right, no matter how long he stood, despairing, in a late-night pharmacy. I'll share an excerpt from her poem "Open Until Midnight" here.

Mary Ann's lovely poem makes me want to cut bad gift-givers some slack. They won't all deserve it, but the man in my life does. He wants to please, but he's not always sure how. Since he's good to me every day, it's not hard to smile at the occasional oddball offering. Take the elephant outfit. (*Take it. Please.*)

.  .  .

from "Open Until Midnight" . . .

*No scent, no glass bottle or shiny silver paper*
*with organza ribbon could tell the depth*
*of his love for the woman—his mother,*
*his lover or his wife. And he'd left the gift*
*buying this long and now had to make a*
     *decision.*
*I wanted to walk up to that man in his work*
     *clothes*
*and say* this one, she'll love this one—*any one*
     *really—*
*so the torment in his eyes and body would cease,*
*he could walk out of that miserable choosing*
*and his large hands could clutch the small*
     *package*
*for the woman waiting for him.*

— Mary Ann Moore

# Momzilla Gets the Blues

I wouldn't say I'm a perfectionist. Not exactly.

I will admit, some people say the old joke—*She walked into a bar, and complained the bar should have been set higher*—may apply to me. I maintain those people are judgy. What mother wouldn't want the wedding of her only daughter to go perfectly? It hardly makes me a Momzilla.

My daughter's wedding was about to take place in scenic Elora, Ontario. The bride-to-be was still at work in California. I'd been running point on this logistical nightmare from our Ontario home: *Wedding Ground Zero*. I was determined to pull off a picture-perfect wedding.

*I can still picture it:*

## Timeline

It is Thursday noon. The bride-to-be (B2B) is to be married in 48 hours. The mother of the bride (MoB) has 68 hours worth of things to do.

## Thursday, 12 p.m.

I return home from shopping, loaded down with purchases, and am relieved to see my husband's car in the driveway. Thank goodness! The father of the bride (FoB) has remembered to take the afternoon off to help.

I rush into our bedroom, toss my purse onto the bed—and watch it fall to the floor, spilling its contents en route. *Unbelievable*. The FoB's idea of helping has been to rearrange the bedroom furniture! There is no bed where the bed should be.

Many people secretly hate change. There is nothing secret about my hatred of all things "new and improved." I loathe change. He knows I loathe change. And when I am running behind and stressed to the nines, introducing change is a very bad idea.

We have words. FoB's are along the lines of "Lighten up— you'll learn to love it." MoB's are unprintable.

## Thursday, 1 p.m.

There is no time to argue. There's far too much to do. The B2B is flying in from L.A. on the Red Eye tonight. I need to wash the sheets in the guest bedroom, so she can grab a few hours' sleep. I check the rest of my "to do" list. Groan.

The FoB repeats, "Lighten up."

Gets the evil eye.

## Friday, 1 a.m.

Most "to-do's" are done. I manage to locate our bed via the sound of FoB's snoring, and fall in, exhausted.

## Friday, 2:00 a.m.

The sound of our basset hounds barking at the squeak of the front door opening alerts me that the B2B has arrived. I grab my robe, rush to hush the dogs—and run directly into the sharp corner of the mahogany wardrobe.

A wardrobe that was never in my path. Until yesterday.

The room spins. The sleepy B2B is greeted by a cacophony of barks and screams, screams and barks.

## Friday, 3:00 a.m.

An hour of ice on my eye and cheekbone confirms the worst. The MoB will have a black eye.

Did I mention the part about how I hate change?

I wail at my husband: "Think of the wedding pictures! The mother of the bride will be wearing a $400 sapphire satin gown —and a shiner!"

"Lighten up," says my change-loving optimist. "It'll be better by then."

I do the math. A black eye, healed in 33 hours? In what universe?

## Saturday, 7:00 a.m. (Wedding Day)

The eye has morphed into a ghastly greenish-purple. "It's neon!" I shriek.

The FoB attempts a "something borrowed, something black-and-blue" wedding joke. It is poorly received.

## Saturday, 9:30 a.m.

The B2B has arranged an emergency makeup session for her mom at the ironically named "Tranquility Spa." By 10:00 a.m., the maternal eye is a minty greenish-mauve—the best that can be hoped for, given the palette in question. Everyone is at pains to assure the MoB it will never show in the photos.

No one mentions that the makeup is half an inch thick and certain to crack like parched soil in a rain shower should the MoB cry—as mothers of the bride are known to do.

Everyone maintains it was a beautiful wedding. The photos confirm it. The bride smiled brightly. The bride's mother smiled bravely. In the right light, that indigo eye might even be taken for a reflection from her sapphire satin gown.

Whenever I look through the wedding album, I must admit that I survived it. Which goes to show that even I can survive change.

But change hurts. Sometimes it leaves you black and blue. Sometimes mint and mauve. Still, you can always laugh. Even I can laugh. Just don't tell me to lighten up.

# END OF LIFE
## Aging, Death, That's All, Folks

# Things I Miss About Being a Kid

P opular wisdom says I should get content with aging—accept where I am right now, and enjoy the rest of the ride. I entirely agree. *And yet* . . . there are things I miss about being a kid. I don't know what you miss, but:

## I miss my tree

There was an old tree by what was then a dump which was an easy climb, even for a klutzy kid like me. I would sit in the crotch of that tree and watch the world go by. It was my—Otis Redding, *"sittin' on the dock of the bay, wastin' time"*—place.

Time was ticking away back then too, but I was oblivious. Maybe what I miss is not my tree. It's being oblivious. Care-free.

## I miss my grandma

She was a seamstress and a saint. She made me and my girl-cousins dresses, never needing a pattern. Instead, she would "feel us up"—much to our embarrassment—and somehow know, from her pinches, pokes, and squeezes, how to fashion a perfectly fitting dress.

When dementia stole her away, she would still sit, meticulously folding, unfolding, and re-folding the same old tea towel —connecting, and loving, through her hands. I miss those hands.

## I miss Mighty Mouse

Animation has advanced by light-years. Still, I'd love to slip back to the simplicity of a 1950s Saturday morning, sitting cross-legged in front of our Philco TV set, getting jam all over my pj's, while Mighty Mouse crows: *"Here I come to save the day!"*

The first innocence-shattering images I recall viewing through that same TV screen were of the failed landing operation at the Bay of Pigs. And how many millions of sad images have we all viewed since? Oh, for a Mighty Mouse to save the day.

## I miss pork hocks and pigtails

I come from Ontario's Waterloo County—a region whose culinary past is Germanic and Pennsylvania Dutch. You won't find pigtails or smoked pork hocks (*schwein shaxe*) with sauerkraut on any menu within thousands of miles of Vancouver Island, where I live now.

Vegetarians will be appalled, but these—along with foods like "cook cheese" (*koch kaese*) and my mother's Amish classic "Apple Grunt" dessert, are the comfort foods of my youth. Just the thought of them takes me back.

## I miss dancing on daddy's feet

. . . and hearing my mother play "Que Sera, Sera" on the piano. *Que* será, será: what will be, will be.

Who knew, back then, what would be? But what *IS*— now, at age 73—is actually fine with me. I am content.

And yet. These things, I miss.

# Waking Up After 70

I woke up with a leg pain
Something wasn't right
The ligament that went to bed
had twisted overnight

I hoped that it could weight-bear,
support me through my day,
but when I tried to stand up
that charley horse said: "NEIGH."

I dropped onto the mattress
to study my condition—
I wasn't giving up yet,
just taking intermission—

I scanned my other members
and my digestive tract;
wiggled all my digits—
most were still intact

*My bladder was insisting*
*I make it down the hall;*
*I gave my leg an order:*
"If necessary, crawl!"

*That leg protested loudly,*
*but held me, even so*
*I made it to the throne room*
*and let Niagara flow*

*Tomorrow might bring toothache*
*or floaters in my eyes—*
*when waking after 70*
*each day holds a surprise*

*This body that has carried me*
*three score and ten-ish years*
*announces every morning:*
Notice me! I'm here!!

*All my parts and pieces*
*take turns at being sore*
*but each a.m. affliction*
proclaims: You've one day more!

# The Decline of the Right

Last week I got a sliver in my heel. Naturally, it was my right heel.

Afflictions glom onto my right side like bees honing in on a honeypot. I'd just returned from having an MRI on my wonky right knee, a knee which must carry me to my upcoming ophthalmologist appointment for my ailing right eye.

Last year, I endured a right-side jaw joint (TMJ) lock-up. And just last month, a bone spur bloomed out of my right clavicle, forming a knob on which I can now hang my tea towel.

What on earth is going on? Am I aging *unevenly*? No one issue is super-serious, but the decline of "the right" is getting me down.

My heel sliver was the last straw (although technically it wasn't a straw, it was a speck of wire). I limped to my laptop and fired up Dr. Google. *Is LOPSIDED aging a thing?* I demanded to know.

It turns out that, yes, there *is* such a thing as asymmetrical aging. Google initially goofed, popping up photos of facial asymmetry (sides of faces that don't mirror each other due to issues like Bell's palsy or stroke).

Then, since I'd asked about asymmetrical *aging*, it threw in some photos of faces doctored with face-aging software. One side of each face was young; the other half was "well-weathered."

Distracted, I immediately needed to experiment with "aging" my own face. I grabbed my best "Before" shot—a "Glamour shot" taken in a local mall kiosk decades ago. Then I downloaded an app called *Face App*, and "aged" the right side of my "Glamour" face. Yikes!

Don't try this at home unless you have a soothing adult beverage at hand.

Onscreen aging was fascinating, but my present-day face actually looks pretty evenly aged. (Like a well-aged cheese. Picture a nice Gouda, with a neck of softened Brie.) None of this explained why the left side of my body thrives, while my right side is a rapidly aging affliction-magnet.

I dug a little deeper, and found one fascinating possible explanation. *I could be a human chimera!* No less an authority than *Scientific American* confirms that human "chimeras"—people who have two unique sets of DNA—can exist.

Chimeras can happen naturally if a fetus absorbs its dead fraternal twin. "These individuals don't know they are a chimera," says *Scientific American*.

I immediately self-diagnosed as a human chimera. What a relief to be able to blame my lousy right-side mojo on my terrible twin! I've had this loser riding shotgun for 70 years! If only she'd kept her bad DNA to herself instead of dragging me down, I'd be thriving clear through.

I can hear you scoffing, saying, "That's ridiculous, chimeras are very rare." Easy for you to say. You're probably aging symmetrically. Those of us who are aging *a*symmetrically need answers.

I have mine. That's my story, and I'm sticking to it.

# Stuff: You Can't Take It With You

I've arrived in my seventies with SO MUCH baggage. Do you want a Suzanne Somers' ThighMaster? You're in luck. This contraption hasn't been compressed by my quivering thighs since circa 1990, but it regularly jams up my closet door. It's yours for the taking—and for the quaking.

My kitchen cupboards are spilling over. There's the set of Wedgwood Queensware, a wedding gift from Aunt Florence that has outlasted that marriage—and, sadly, outlasted Aunt Flo as well. The set came complete with an embossed ashtray. I quit smoking in 1981, but should the urge strike, I apparently want an ashtray at hand.

Then there's the miniature teacup embossed with tiny shamrocks that seemed like such a find at the time. Turns out very few Irish leprechauns ever stop by for a cuppa. The dratted thing is forever getting knocked over when I reach for dessert plates.

I know it's time to pare down. Should I pass my "treasures" along to the next generation? "Over my dead body," says my daughter, horrified at the thought of my kitsch cluttering up her cupboards or clashing with her decor.

A friend suggests I read a book called *The Gentle Art of Swedish Death Cleaning*. The "D" word gives me a chill. Is *that* why I've avoided disposing of my stuff? If I clear away my clutter, will the Grim Reaper somehow be notified? I'M NOT READY!

I am also not a hoarder. Well, not exactly. I'm not as bad as Dan Regan who recently tweeted, "One day I may need a Sega Genesis controller and a 1983 Trapper Keeper." I am proud to say I own neither. And yet—there is a Sony Walkman with earmuff-size headphones that's lived in my bedside table since the early 80s. *Busted.*

Okay, I am clearly more of a hoarder than a "tosser." Jerry Seinfeld is a tosser. Not a tosser in the British English slang sense of being an obnoxious jerk. A tosser because he maintains:

> All things on earth only exist in different stages of becoming garbage.
>
> — Jerry Seinfeld

Jerry says he loves throwing out garbage. In fact, he says he finds that once he has something, he no longer wants it.

Jerry would make an awesome Scandinavian death cleaner. Me, not so much. There are memories encased in my bric-a-brac that might not mean much to you, but seem to still matter to me.

I was once that woman who craved Suzanne Somers-style thighs and blasted Bonnie Tyler's "Total Eclipse of the Heart" through that very Walkman. It will hurt my heart a little to let her go.

Still, the time has come to make a start on paring down my paraphernalia. It's a daunting task. But today I read that renowned TV pitchman and gadget-guy, Ron Popeil, has passed away. I picture his garage — possibly stacked to the ceiling with unsold Veg-O-Matics, Hav-A-Maid Mops and Inside-the-Eggshell Egg Scramblers.

Things could always be worse.

# Leave 'em Laughing

Sooner or later, you'll shuffle off this mortal coil. Your obituary offers you one last chance to stand out from the crowd. Slip in a hilarious zinger, and you might even go viral!

Not sure how to turn your "In Memoriam" into an "In Hilariam?" Match your nearest personality prototype below, and model your farewell after one of these actual viral obits. They were scooped from local newspapers, shared on sites like *Twitter* (now *X*), *Reddit*, *BuzzFeed* and *Today.com.*, and read by millions:

## Got a grievance to get off your chest (or other body part)?

Model your obit after Chan Holcombe's. Chan's obituary states he was born in a log cabin in Bates, where he "was circumcised with his dad's pocket knife." Ouch. Possibly TMI, Chan, but we now feel we know you well.

## Got a political point to make?

Slip it in slyly, like Mike Blanchard did. Mike's "In Memoriam" pointed out that many of his childhood friends had "gone on to become criminals, prostitutes or Democrats."

## Unsure about your politics? Skip out.

Model William Ziegler, whose obituary (penned by his kids) states, "He escaped this mortal realm on July 29, 2016—on purpose, to avoid having to make a decision in the pending presidential election."

## Got a pet peeve?

Here's your chance to complain! Copy Robert F. Gibson, whose obituary stated he was from northern Virginia, and said he hated, "how all of you were incapable of driving competently."

## Need to mend some fences?

Slip in an apology. Emily Philips used her obit to say she was sorry for making her daughter Bonnie wear No Frills jeans when she was little and for "red-shirting" her son Scott in kindergarten.

"Apparently, each of these things was humiliating to them," she acknowledged, "but both were able to rise above their shame and become very successful adults." Nice recovery, Emily.

## Worn out? Fed up? Speak up!

Mary "Pat" Stocks's obituary laid the blame for her heart failure where she deemed it belonged. Her obit said her cause of death was believed to be "from carrying her oxygen tank up the long flight of stairs to her bedroom."

## Hate gawkers?

So did Angus MacDonald. His obit shared his discomfort with the idea of people, "gawking at me as I lie in a coffin." Instead of "going to see the creator," he said he'd be going to see "the cremator." Angus's obit speculated that his ashes would be kept around, "as long as they matched the décor." Tasteful.

## Regrets, you've had a few? Spell them out.

James Groth's self-penned obit said his regrets were few—but he did regret "eating a rotisserie hot dog from a convenience store in the summer of 2002." He further regretted in print that, "no video evidence exists of his prowess on the soccer field or in the bedroom." Hot dawg, James!

## Are you the last to go?

Many an obituary states that the deceased was preceded in death by a sibling or spouse. Walter Bruhl, Jr.'s obit went further. It states he was "preceded in death by his tonsils and adenoids in 1935, a spinal disc in 1974, a large piece of his thyroid gland in 1988, and his prostate on March 27th, 2000." Death by a thousand cuts.

## Proud of your ride? Point it out.

The obituary of muscle car owner "Lucky Lorne" said he "leaves behind a 1974 Trans Am 450 Turbo, and four estranged kids." Not being Dad of the Year didn't seem to bother Lorne. His obit said his greatest accomplishment was "forcing his 1974 Trans Am over 150 miles an hour down the Port Alberni stretch."

## Are you a foodie? Spill your secrets.

Harry Weathersby Stamps shared the sources for his signature bacon and tomato sandwich: "100% all-white Bunny Bread from Georgia, Blue Plate mayonnaise from New Orleans, Sauer's black pepper from Virginia, homegrown tomatoes from outside Oxford, and Tennessee's Benton bacon from his bacon-of-the-month subscription." You don't have a bacon-of-the-month subscription? Step up your game.

## Animal lover? State your preferences.

Holly Blair's obit states she was survived by "four spoiled cats, two stinky dogs, three bad birds, a turtle and an utterly useless frog named Fred, as well as three children and a husband of little to no importance." Even the "useless" frog got named. Sorry, hubby.

## Cat got your tongue?

Maybe you're a man of few words, like Douglas Legler. If so, get right to the point. Doug did. Beneath his photo, his obit simply read:
    "Doug died."

# To My Husband, To Be Read in the Event That I Predecease You

*If you're reading this, I've predeceased you*
*Which sucks for me. But I now release you:*
*I declare herein: You may marry again.*
*But NOT TOO SOON. So the question is: When?*

*Certainly not within a year*
*I want to make that totally clear.*
*If I've just been reduced to ashes and cinder*
*Don't even THINK of going on Tinder.*

*At 18 months, you could start your search —*
*Maybe scope out a widow from our church:*
*Definitely not Donna Dean*
*or you'll have to live on Lean Cuisine.*

*You deserve to be a happy man*
*which you'd never be with Fay McCann*
*or Brenda Burk. She's a real disaster.*
*For better options, ask the pastor.*

*If all else fails, get off the sofa*
*Join a bowling league, or try out yoga.*
*Wait! Yoga ladies, they can flex,*
*so they might give you better sex—*

*NO! That's where I must draw the line:*
*The BEST sex must be yours and mine!*
*So when it's time to get things rolling*
*Skip the yoga! Stick to bowling!*

*A woman who throws strikes and spares*
*and likes your jokes, and really cares—*
*Someone who's not too depressing:*
*That sort of wife would have my blessing.*

*Yours Eternally,*
*xoxo*
*P.S. I mean it about the yoga. I WILL KNOW.*[1]

# Other Than That, I'm Fine

You know the type: the cocktail party bore who just has to get in the last word. Some funnier folks carry this compulsion to the grave— and come up with hilarious epitaphs on their tombstones.

Sites like *Pinterest, Twitter* and *Reddit* often carry photos of funny tombstones. I've scoured a few such online "cemeteries" and "unearthed" a few of my personal favourites:

## I'm dead. Other than that, I'm fine

Catholic priest Father James Mallon says his dad, Ronnie, always joked he wanted the above words on his gravestone. His son put that comment on his dad's grave marker. "It's funny, it feels like him, and it's a Glaswegian reflection on 1 Cor 15:55."

> Where, O death, is your victory? Where, O death, is your sting?"
>
> — 1 Corinthians 15:55

Not everyone was as "fine" with the finality of their situation as the upbeat Ronnie Mallon. The headstone of one annoyed fellow with the surname Mitchell complains, "**WELL, THIS SUCKS**." (*Twitter*)

Lola S. Holt took a more stoical view. She shuffled off this mortal coil at age 81 with an uncomplaining "**OH, WELL, WHATEVER**" epitaph engraved on her headstone. (*Pinterest*)

## I told you I was sick

One couple that must have been a riot at parties share a headstone sporting dual epitaphs. His plaque reads: "**I TOLD YOU I WAS SICK**." Hers retorts: "**AND I WAS SICK OF HEARING IT**." (*Reddit*)

Those aren't the only complainers. Some of the departed aren't happy with their current accommodation. One claustrophobic joker grumbles: "**DAMN, IT'S DARK DOWN HERE**." (*Find a Grave*)

A woman who demanded her personal space in life insists on nothing less now. An inscription on the lower right of her tombstone reads, "**IF YOU CAN READ THIS, YOU'RE STANDING ON MY BOOBS**." Ouch. (*Reddit.*)

And isn't there always that one "entitled" dude? In life, he had to have the penthouse. In death, he fumes:

## Entertaining sign offs

One witty fellow had to wait his whole life to make use of his awesome exit line: "**HERE LIES JOHN YEAST. PARDON ME FOR NOT RISING**." (*Bored Panda*)

The professional entertainers weren't to be outdone. TV game show host Merv Griffin's epitaph quips: "**I WILL *NOT* BE BACK AFTER THIS MESSAGE**." (*Pinterest*)

Comedian Rodney Dangerfield—known in life for his line, "I don't get no respect"—suspects he won't get much in his new locale either. His headstone reads: "**THERE GOES THE NEIGHBORHOOD**." (*Pinterest*)

The last word goes to Mel Blanc, the American voice-over artist known as "the man of a thousand voices." He famously voiced cartoon characters like Bugs Bunny and Daffy Duck. Blanc's epitaph quotes the exit line of his beloved Porky Pig character:

*Th-Th-The, Th-Th-The, Th-Th**THAT'S ALL, FOLKS***

. . . and indeed, *that's all, folks*—for me too. Thank you for reading! This is really and truly

THE END.

# Acknowledgments

My sincere thanks to my early readers, Cindy Shantz and Judy Mayhew, for their candid, constructive feedback (*OMG, leave THAT out!*). Any writer would be blessed to count two such bright lights among their dear friends. Luckily, I found them first!

Thanks also to my "wardrobe crew." It took Ruth's umbrella, Cindy's raincoat, Diana's boots and Barbara Anne's fabulous photography to capture that cover image.

Thanks also to my indulgent husband, Randy, who continues to feed and spoil me—even when I spoof his gaffes and blunders. Most of all, my thanks to you, dear readers and audience members, for your continued encouragement!

Laughter is a gift best shared. If you enjoyed this book, please tell a friend or post a positive review online. Word of mouth matters. Of course, if you hated it, *mum's the word*. #KIDDING. Feel free to speak your truth. I'll be crushed, but other than that, I'll be fine.

*Judy*

Website judymillar.ca
Facebook judy.millar.77
Instagram @judymillarpix
Medium @judymillar
X (Twitter) @judymillar

# Video Performances

- Portions of "My Life as a 'Live Wire" can be viewed on YouTube. Click (or search by name) Judy Millar's "Trailer Factory Screw-up" and "Conveyor Belt Klutz."
- Judy's presentation of the script from "Your Call Is (he, he) Important To Us" is on YouTube. Click (or search by name) "Judy Millar - The Automated Lady."
- Judy's presentation of the essay "Kissing for Klutzes" can be viewed on YouTube. Click (or search by name) "Kissing for Klutzes."
- Judy's presentation of the essay "You Got Me . . . WHAT??" can be viewed on YouTube. Click (or search by name) Judy Millar's "You Got Me WHAT?".
- Judy's presentation of the essay "Momzilla Gets the Blues" can be viewed on YouTube. Click (or search by name) Judy Millar - Mother of the Bride."

# Images

The author gratefully acknowledges the following creators/sources for the photos and images used to illustrate these essays:

- "Breathe Like Brenda" *Photo of Sleepless Woman* Jen Theodore on Unsplash
- "Hey, Chuck Gobnik" *Illustration of Newscaster* Mohamed Hassan on Pixabay, modified by author
- "Your Call Is (he he) Important to Us" *Illustration of Skeleton* Andrew Fraser @cartoonsidrew
- "Eve's Manifesto" *Adam and Eve* OpenClipart-Vectors from Pixabay
- "An Open Letter to CAPTCHA and reCAPTCHA" *CAPTCHA / reCAPTCHA* Author's drawing of screen image
- "Bite Me" *Hamburger* Clker-Free-Vector-Images from Pixabay, modified by author
- "'Tis The Season" *Judy: The Christmas Elephant* Author's photo

- "Famous Philosophers Meet on Zoom" *Computer Monitor Zoom Meeting Screen* everesd_design from Pixabay, Daniela Ruiz from Pexels and various Wiki (Fair Use), altered
- "Are Bubonic Remedies Right for You?" *Woodcut of Flagellants,* 1493. Public domain from the Nuremberg Chronicles by Hartmann Schedel via Wikipedia
- "Historical Online Dating Profiles" *Henry VIII on Cell Phone* Art by Kyrie Gray on *Medium*, used by permission
- "Shakespeare's Characters Contemplate Wearing a Mask" *Lady Macbeth* Art by Kyrie Gray on *Medium*, used by permission
- "Auf Wiedersehen, Ludwig" *Beethoven* Image by Clker-Free-Vector-Images from Pixabay
- "Birds, Bees & Limericks, Please" *Bumble bee* Image by Clker-Free-Vector-Images from Pixabay
- "Waking Up After 70" *Wooden Physio Doll* Photo by Paul Seling in Pexels, modified by author
- "To My Husband, To Be Read in the Event That I Predecease You" *Woman in Yoga Pose* Photo by Alex Shaw on Unsplash, modified by author
- "Other Than That, I'm Fine" *Tombstone* Image by OpenClipart-Vectors on Pixabay (altered by author)

# Notes

## My Eye Guy is On To Me

1. Pac-Man is the Trademark and official mascot of Bandai Namco Entertainment, Inc.

## On Searching for Your Mobile Phone

1. After Brian Bilston's poem, "On Searching for a Book of Stamps"

## To My Husband, To Be Read in the Event That I Predecease You

1. After Scott Hughey's essay, "To My Wife, Upon the Occasion of my Death"

# Previous Publication Credits

The essay "Kissing for Klutzes" was first published in 2018 in the anthology *Flash Nonfiction Funny*, Woodhall Press.

The poems "Waking Up After 70," "Half-baked Barista" and "To My Husband, To Be Read in the Event That I Predecease You" were first published in print in 2023 in the anthology *Laugh Lines,* Repartee Press.

Portions of some essays in this book were previously published in the following online publications under the following titles.

**In all cases, copyright remains with the author.**

***The Haven:*** "Fitbitten: Who, Me?"; "Half-baked Barista"; "Your Call Is (he, he) Important to Us"; "I'm a Chick Magnet for Hot Babes from Russia"; "Bidet, Mate! Potty Talk for the Post-Apocalypse"; "Things Brad Pitt and I Have In Common"; "Here's Looking at U, Whoever U R."

***No Crime in Rhymin':*** "Limericks, Starbucks-style!"; "On Searching for Your Mobile Phone"; "The Birds and The Bees — Limericks, Please!"

***Medium:*** "Insulted? Snappy Comebacks You Can Use To Stand Up For Yourself"; "Birds, Bees and Fleas Do It."

***MuddyUm:*** "Eve's Manifesto"; "Hey Morgan Freeman, Can You Bark Like a Dog?"; "I Am Not a Bot, You Bastards"; "Bite Me"; "The Meaning of Life According to Siri"; "I've Been a 'Live Wire' and a Dead Chicken-Handler"; "An Insomniac Overthinker Attempts Alternate Nostril Breathing"; "Six Surprising Facts About Your Body"; "Hey, Chuck Gopnik: Stop Mispronouncing the N-word"; "An Open Letter to the Cliché Cops in My Writing Group"; "An Ode to Parentheticals."

***Hope\*Healing\*Humour:*** "These Christmas Gifts Were Ho-Ho-Horrible."

***Slackjaw:*** "Famous Philosophers' Zoom Meeting Goes Sideways."

***Jane Austen's Wastebasket***: "Are Bubonic Remedies Right for You?"; "Famous Historical Figures Draft their Online Dating Profiles"; "Being Shakespeare's Wife is Not Easy"; "Shakespeare's Characters Contemplate Wearing a Mask"; "William Wordsworth's Ex Rewrites 'I Wandered Lonely as a Cloud'."

***Crow's Feet:*** "My Eye Guy is On To Me"; "How We Got to Be Smokin' Hot Babes (and Legends in Our Own Minds)"; "Marriage: It's Mostly Saying, "It's Wherever You Left It.""; "Things I Miss About Being a Kid"; "Waking Up After 70 — Yow! What Now?!!"; "Are You Aging Asymmetrically? This Might Be Why"; "Stuff: You Can't Take It With You"; "To My Husband, To Be Read in the Event That I Predecease You"; "Funny Actual Epitaphs: They Got in the Last Word."

***The Memoirist:*** "Disaster at the Drive-In: My First Kiss."

**P.S. I Love You:** "How I Made My Guy More Romantic"; "When Your Great Guy is a Bad Gift-Giver; You got me . . . WHAT??."

**Inspired Writer:** "Momzilla Gets the (Something Borrowed, Something) Blues."

# About the Author

Judy Millar is a writer and comedic storyteller. She's been published in *The Globe and Mail, Reader's Digest, Writer's Digest,* and in anthologies like *Laugh Lines* and *Flash Nonfiction Funny.* Her first book was *Beaver Bluff, The Librarian Stories.* She lives on beautiful Vancouver Island, where she's been known to engage in comedic storytelling, clumsy kayaking and lively line dancing—but not all at once.

Manufactured by Amazon.ca
Bolton, ON

40902163R00105